D0537115

Joe Clark
The Emerging Leader

by Michael Nolan
with photographs by
Ted Grant

Fitzhenry & Whiteside
Toronto   Montreal   Winnipeg   Vancouver

To my wife Carole and my parents,
Michael and Gertrude Mary Nolan

M.N.

To my wife Irene,
who opened the door to photography

T.G.

© Fitzhenry & Whiteside Limited 1978

All rights reserved

No part of this publication may be
reproduced in any form, or by any
means, without permission in writing
from the publisher.

Fitzhenry & Whiteside Limited
150 Lesmill Road,
Don Mills, Ontario M3B 2T5

Canadian Cataloguing in Publication Data

Nolan, Michael.
  Joe Clark: The Emerging Leader.

ISBN 0-88902-436-7

1. Clark, Joe, 1939—   2. Politicians –
Canada – Biography.

FC626.C53N64   971.06′44′0924   C78-001135-X
F1034.3.C53N64

Printed and bound in Canada

Contents

Preface

The idea for this book originated with Robert Fitzhenry, who wanted a photo-biography to capture a day in the life of a federal party leader in Canada. Arrangements for a book of this nature could not be finalized with the Prime Minister's Office. The Conservative party, on the other hand, was willing to provide the necessary access so that a portrait of a party leader in action could be presented. Eventually it was decided to broaden the book's scope to include the human dimensions of the office of the leader of the opposition — to show a party leader's problems and shortcomings as well as his aspirations and triumphs.

It should be emphasized that the book is not intended to be a conventional biography. The collaboration between Ted Grant and myself was aimed primarily at producing a volume of words and pictures which would give the reader some insight into Joe Clark the man and the possible future prime minister of Canada. In no sense is the book definitive; rather it is a profile of the man in action.

A great many people have made this book possible. As even a glimpse at the text will reveal, special gratitude must go to the leader of the opposition and his wife Maureen. Without their cooperation and willingness to make their time available to me, a book of this kind would have been impossible.

Thanks must also go to Walter Baker, Elmer MacKay, Steve Paproski, Ray Hnatyshyn and Ian Green, all of whom had to grow accustomed to my attendance at the House leaders' meetings. Bill Neville, the leader's chief of staff, was particularly helpful in arranging for access to caucus, as was

Murray Coolican, who helped launch the project, and Lowell Murray, who was always willing to discuss with me his recollections of Joe Clark from the early 1960s onward. Ms. Jodi White, Clark's director of communications, patiently withstood my continual prodding to open yet another door for still closer access to the leader, and the rest of Joe Clark's staff responded promptly to my constant requests.

The following members of the Conservative caucus were generous in granting me interview time: Jim Gillies, Douglas Roche, Harvie Andre, Sinclair Stevens, Bill Jarvis, John Wise and Bruce Halliday. In High River, Joe Clark's parents, Mr. and Mrs. Charles Clark, consented to answer numerous questions about their son's early life. Appreciation is also extended to Don Tanner, Jim Howie, Norman Ray, Penny Wallace and Jeannette Rousseau in High River and Calgary; Donald Matthews and Peter White in London, Ontario; Trevor Jones in Kitchener-Waterloo; John Grace, editorial editor of the *Ottawa Journal*; and Norman Atkins, Dalton Camp and John Morand in Toronto.

The staffs of the Edmonton and London public libraries helped garner essential information, and the library staff of the *Albertan* in Calgary allowed me to delve into their newspaper files on Joe Clark's earlier political years. Diane Mew, a thorough and skilful editor, helped greatly with her wise counsel. I am also indebted to the Ontario Arts Council for a grant toward the project.

Dr. Stuart Selby, the former chairman of the Communication Studies Department at the University of Windsor, kindly relieved me of regular duties to allow time for research, as did Andrew MacFarlane, Dean of the School of Journalism at the University of Western Ontario, so that the manuscript could be completed. Finally, I would like to thank Peter Neary and Paul Crunican, of the history department at Western, who have taught me a great deal about Canadian political history. Responsibility for all errors and omissions rests with the author.

Michael Nolan
London, Ontario
February, 1978

A Note from the Photographer

It would have been impossible for me to produce the photographs in this book without the cooperation and help of a great many people. My thanks must go, in particular, to Joe Clark for his trust and understanding, but most of all for his patience. It must have been trying at times having me in the background, but he never asked me to leave, and only once remarked that he didn't know how long he could cope with having me around. Maureen agreed to all my photographic requests and even allowed me to photograph Catherine Jane the day after she was born.

Thanks are also due to those on the Conservative leader's staff: Jodi White, Wendy Orr, Donald Doyle, Ian Green and the many others who made it possible for me, an outsider, to become an insider.

The photographs of the 1976 leadership convention on pages 10, 11 and 20 were taken by Crombie McNeill and are reproduced here with his permission.

Ted Grant
Ottawa
February 1978

Everybody's Second Choice

They had gathered in convention to choose a new leader, the supreme exercise of political parties: young and old Tories watching the transfer of power within the party to a new generation. Four days of hoedowns, eat-Grits breakfasts, bands and booze had taken their toll on the 2,600 delegates in the nation's capital, there to select the potential successor to Canada's prime minister. Now it was Sunday, 22 February 1976, and the delegates had made their final trek from downtown hotels on Ottawa's snow-covered streets to the Civic Centre, site of the convention.

Above all, this mid-winter convention was a media extravaganza. Television, the power play of politics, recorded the drama and the high points just as it had done some twenty years earlier when the "Chief" had captured the party leadership. Yet the scale of coverage then could not compare with the four television and six radio networks now located throughout the Civic Centre to show the country the gladiators clashing in political combat. A number of the candidates aiming for the title of leader had their first smell of smoke-filled rooms in 1956 when the party, with six leaders since 1919, had chosen John Diefenbaker. Now the Chief was watching as the man who had replaced him gave way to yet another party head.

The moment of truth was at hand after an exhausting four days of soul-searching. The convention was down to the fourth and final ballot. The names of only two candidates remained — Claude Wagner, his supporters with their red, white and blue colours at one end of the arena contrasting sharply with the yellow and black of Joe Clark, the other contender, at the opposite end of the Civic Centre.

Clark addressing the 1976 leadership convention on 21 February, the eve of voting day. "Our strength," he told the delegates, "is that we all reflect where we are from and respect where others come from. My sense of Canada was formed in the open West and has been broadened by a unique opportunity to see this country whole."

Diefenbaker had already bestowed his blessing on Wagner. Would the delegates follow the Chief's example and choose Wagner, a French Canadian and the candidate seemingly aligned with the right wing of the party? Certainly the mood of the convention and the country was favourable to him. Or did they prefer a candidate who would follow more closely in the footsteps of Robert Stanfield, the retiring party leader, who had tried to move the party further to the left? If so, Clark was their man.

The delegates waited. Then came the announcement: Clark, 1,187. Wagner, 1,122. Sixty-five votes. Thirty-three people. Clark, accompanied by his wife Maureen, proceeded onto the stage to be joined by the other

Maureen McTeer — a determined campaigner for her husband.

The waiting is over. On stage at the Civic Centre following the fourth ballot, the new leader embraces his wife.

candidates — except Paul Hellyer who had already gone home after his defeat. Looking fatigued and wearing a yellow daffodil pinned to his lapel, Clark told the delegates they would capture the country "not by storm or stealth or surprise but by hard work." Later came the words which clearly reflected the positive nature of the Clark leadership drive: "The voters don't want to know what we're against, they want to know what we're for." At the age of 36, Charles Joseph Clark had become the seventh leader of the Progressive Conservative party to be chosen in convention and the youngest ever federal party leader in Canadian history.

Clark is fond of saying that he managed to win the leadership of the party because he "was everybody's second choice at the convention." There is truth in those words. Clearly, Clark was the compromise candidate, as journalists have repeatedly reminded us. But it is worth pausing here a moment to see how he emerged as everybody's second choice.

When Trudeaumania swept the land in 1968, the Conservative party suffered a severe setback, mainly in urban Canada. Equally significant for the future of the party was the fact that several senior politicians who had been leadership candidates in the 1967 Conservative convention were defeated, among them Duff Roblin and Davie Fulton. That memorable election campaign in the innocent springtime of 1968 toppled a number of Conservative giants. So Robert Stanfield inherited a party that had no apparent successor when the time came for him to step down. Not surprisingly, most of the leadership hopefuls in 1976, including Joe Clark, had been elected for the first time in 1972. In short, the Conservative party jumped a generation and the Clark campaign, with its obvious emphasis on youth, reflected this leap forward.

The campaign clearly highlighted the candidate's straightforward, positive style. It was not what could be called splashy, but there certainly were touches of class. A politician highly aware of the importance of symbols, Clark and his wife were brought to the Civic Centre prior to his convention speech in an open landau carriage. According to Jim Hawkes, one of Clark's principal organizers, the landau was chosen because Clark was of the opinion that Canadians with an ethnic background expect a kingly appearance. Apparently it was wise strategy; some French-Canadian delegates were later overheard commenting that Clark "looked like a prime minister."

Indeed, the campaign was skilfully organized, but above all it was based on a simple strategy — the emphasis of positive initiatives during

11

meetings between the candidate and groups of party supporters. The campaign was devoid of negative attacks on any other candidate or on Pierre Trudeau. Afterwards, several pundits argued that Clark used the Jimmy Carter approach of meeting small groups of people until his campaign began to gain momentum. "In fact," says Harvie Andre, one of Clark's top campaign organizers, "he preceded Carter. He was doing all this before Carter really started to go." As his opponents for one reason or another became less acceptable to the delegates, Clark was seen eventually as the successor to Robert Stanfield.

Clark's small group of willing amateurs had their Ottawa campaign headquarters in an old Bell Canada office about six blocks from the Convention Centre. His national campaign coordinator, Dave King, explained during convention week that Clark was looking for nothing less than 450 votes on the first ballot. He argued that his candidate's greatest strength lay in the fact that he was the second choice of a lot of people and that Clark had the best-organized campaign. King placed heavy emphasis on the personal contacts coast to coast that Clark had built up through his work in the party.

Moreover, the Clark campaign was not waiting until delegates arrived in Ottawa to greet them with campaign literature. They were passing out pamphlets and brochures at airports in Montreal, Toronto, Halifax and Vancouver as the delegates left for Ottawa. In this way, they had a jump on the other candidates in the race. King also went on to say that the media tended to over-generalize about the leadership candidates and were too quick to put left and right labels on them without examining and understanding their positions. "If you look at social issues," he said, "Joe Clark might be called a progressive. But he also has a strong sense of need for the responsibility of the individual."

Clark's campaign could hardly have been more systematically organized. But the quantity of media exposure he had received, particularly early in the leadership race, had not compared with the amount of attention paid to some of the other candidates. Despite this drawback in public exposure, by early February it was apparent that his campaign had gained momentum. The candidate who many felt was running for "next time" seemed determined to win "this time." By convention week, it was clear that Clark had closed a large gap, because observers who at one time had rated him as a first-round drop-out now placed him with the middle-ground contenders.

Unlike many of his opponents, Clark came to the convention with few liabilities. Claude Wagner, his closest challenger, was an ex-Liberal cabinet minister in the province of Quebec. The handling of a $300,000 trust fund set up for him by the Conservative party left question marks in the minds of many delegates.

The computer candidate at the convention was Brian Mulroney, a Montreal lawyer who had gained prominence in Quebec as a member of the three-man Cliche Commission into violence in the construction industry. His smile, resonant voice and overall demeanour gave him a presence at the convention the other candidates, with the possible exception of Wagner, seemed to lack. Most important of all, Mulroney was fluently bilingual and, in the eyes of his followers, the candidate who could oppose Pierre Trudeau most effectively. Yet, regardless of how many times the computer was fed, the printout continued to point to a glaring weakness in Mulroney's candidacy: he had never before run for public office and, despite his many years of service to the party as a backroom organizer, he remained untried and unproven as a campaigner.

Mulroney's supporters were a curiously hybrid bunch. His campaign consisted of youthful party members looking for a quick victory at the polls and representatives from Canada's business community such as Don McDougall, president of Labatt Breweries, the company that had acquired the Toronto Blue Jays baseball team. McDougall, who had attended St. Dunstan's (now the University of Prince Edward Island) in Charlottetown, had debated against Mulroney when the candidate was a student at St. Francis Xavier in Antigonish, Nova Scotia. On the surface, the two groups appeared to have little in common. Seldom is the exuberance of youth combined with the pragmatism of financiers. However, a single unifying element held them together — namely, the belief that Mulroney's suave manner could lead the party to victory in the next federal election. Yet, in the final analysis, what finished Mulroney was the association he seemed to have with big business, in particular the Power Corporation headed by his friend Paul Desmarais, whose company contributed $10,000 to the Mulroney campaign.

After the convention Peter White, a key organizer for Mulroney, claimed that his opponents used the Power Corporation and Mulroney's association with Desmarais to tar the candidate "with the brush of big business." White, a lawyer and publisher in London, Ontario, was a former aide to Wagner and joined Mulroney because he felt Wagner would be vulnerable as party leader, given the manner in which he had handled the controversial trust fund. "Brian had a lot of contacts in the business community," White said, "but it was not a coalition of big business that got behind him. Businessmen got behind Brian because they like to back a winner and I don't think there is any more to it than that."

Although it was clear at the end of convention week and after the candidates' speeches that Mulroney's campaign had slowed down, his organizers remained convinced he would be the victor. Not surprisingly, as voting proceeded and the convention began to coalesce around Clark and Wagner, pandemonium gripped the Mulroney section at the Civic Centre, and his workers in the command booths at the top of the arena became almost hysterical in shouting directions to their colleagues on the convention floor. "These guys in the command booths could not believe it," White recalled. "They were screaming through their microphones at various people on the floor in desperation to do this or that hoping to pull off a miracle and get more support to Mulroney." But the candidate's workers had nowhere to turn. The Mulroney campaign had inflated and deflated as Joe Clark had anticipated.

Undoubtedly, Flora MacDonald's entry into the leadership race hurt Mulroney's chances. He had hoped that support would come from her because of their close friendship over the years. Mulroney also wanted New Brunswick's Premier Richard Hatfield on his side. But his dreams were shattered when Flora decided to seek the leadership herself and won the support of Hatfield. She staged an impressive populist campaign but really had three strikes against her. One was the simple fact that she was a woman asking the Conservative party to be a shade trendy and choose a female leader. The country was not quite ready for this kind of invitation. Secondly, as the member for Kingston and the Islands, she faced the same problem as the other Ontario candidates — the realization that the base of the party had shifted away from their province to the west. Thirdly, within the caucus, some of the more conventional right-wing members worried about the public perception of her as a Red Tory: at the simplest level, a Conservative who prefers the NDP to the Liberals. Some southern Ontario caucus members and western MPs were not comfortable with her stand on certain issues, such as capital punishment and abortion. When the first ballot returns were in, her followers were stunned when she finished sixth with only 214 votes.

Clearly, they had been disillusioned. Something like a hundred delegates did not live up to their commitment to her and, as journalist Harry Bruce concluded, "it's doubtful if more than one-twentieth of the 600-odd women delegates voted for Flora."

On the opening ballot, Flora found herself even behind Horner and Hellyer. "Clark beat her by 63 votes," Bruce wrote, "and because she was now a clear loser, the second-ballot strength she'd once counted on getting flowed to him. She hung on for the second ballot, partly to prove she was not just the token woman among the candidates, picked up 25 more votes, and moved to Clark herself."

The dramatic stroll which Flora took down the convention floor to the Clark section at the Civic Centre was an agonizing few minutes for the Mulroney campaign. Mulroney felt that possibly Flora would give her support to him if she were forced to withdraw from the leadership race early. But Flora led her supporters directly to Clark who greeted her with open arms — it was undoubtedly one of the convention's high points. "Flora had to walk right past Brian to get to Clark at the end, " Peter White remembers, "and she did so with her head high and not looking right or left and I think that was tough. We really had some hope we could get some converts and not one of them came."

The campaign of former Liberal Paul Hellyer had moved ahead steadily and toward the middle of convention week he appeared to be a strong contender. Veteran of twenty-five years of political experience, Hellyer impressed many delegates with his performance at the policy sessions at the Skyline Hotel. A solid speech to the convention, it was felt, would solidify his position and even add to the growing list of delegates committed to him. Certainly, victory was within his grasp. However, it was his speech to the delegates that put an end to his political career, probably forever. Above all, the delegates to this convention were determined to show the country they were united and that the ideological split in the party was grossly exaggerated. When Hellyer attacked the "Red Tories," he underlined the very rift the party had tried to play down before the all-seeing eye of the television camera. There were loud boos when Hellyer remarked that he had seen "Red Tories going the same way Trudeau was going and where the NDP had been." The remark was a giant blunder and clearly showed that Hellyer had failed to measure the mood of the party and the convention. At that moment, Hellyer's campaign for the leadership ended abruptly.

What puzzled so many observers was how a seasoned campaigner like Hellyer could have committed such a tactical error at a convention where party unity was unquestionably the dominant theme. Perhaps a partial answer can be found in the style of campaign Hellyer staged in his drive for the leadership. Jim Gillies, another leadership candidate, recalls that Hellyer chose not to attend any of the all-candidates' meetings. "That is what really sunk him," according to Gillies, "because if Paul had shown up at any one of those meetings he would have known that there was one theme at the convention and that was party unity." Hellyer had decided to conduct his own campaign apart from the other candidates. "Vancouver, Calgary, Toronto and Halifax, that was where all the candidates' meetings were," says Gillies, "if he had gone to one, he never would have made that speech." Donald Matthews, a former national president of the party and a key organizer for Hellyer, could not believe the speech when he heard it. "I was sure we had the convention," Matthews said, "until that speech."

In retrospect, Hellyer has to assume full responsibility for his miscue, because he violated the wishes of the campaign workers closest to him. Two days before the speeches were to be delivered to the convention, Matthews asked Hellyer for a copy of the speech he planned to give. The former Liberal cabinet minister read the speech to his organizers and the people around him on Friday, the day before all candidates addressed the convention. Matthews and several other supporters were disappointed with the first draft. In their eyes, the speech did not strike a high enough tone. So it was redrafted and Hellyer agreed to look at it the following morning.

At the Friday night meeting, the Red Tory faction in the party had been thoroughly discussed. While some Hellyer supporters saw advantage for their candidate in challenging that wing of the party, the meeting decided unanimously that there was to be no mention of Red Tories in the speech. Therefore Hellyer's assault on the progressives in the party in his speech startled Matthews, because it came as such a surprise. "Our instructions were not followed," Matthews says, "he has to take responsibility." Hellyer received 231 votes on the first ballot but dropped to 118 on the second. His staying on clearly hurt Wagner's chances. But it was his speech that had done the damage and helped Clark to emerge as the eventual winner.

To some extent Gillies, along with the other hopefuls — Heward Graff-tey, John Fraser, Patrick Nowlan and Sinclair Stevens — suffered from one fundamental problem: the lack of a broad political base. In a sense, Clark also had this problem. But while he had no clear hold on any section of the country, he had a sprinkling of backers right across Canada. In time, these small patches of support came together to give him the leadership.

And so it turned out on that momentous Sunday afternoon when the voting began. On the first ballot Clark finished third, with 277 votes. Fellow Albertan Jack Horner made a surprisingly strong showing, with 235 votes. This strength was not maintained, however, on the second ballot. When Horner polled only 286 votes, his campaign came to an end and he counselled his supporters to vote for Wagner.

Sinclair Stevens undoubtedly was the candidate who shifted the momentum of the convention towards Clark after the first ballot. The son of an Irish immigrant who came to Canada in 1924, Stevens became a prosperous Toronto financier before entering politics. Above all else, Stevens is an intensely practical man. After his seventh place finish on the first ballot, he realized it was futile to remain in the race. Stevens' campaign organizers had conducted a private poll during convention week and expected something like 300 votes on the opening ballot compared to the 182 which they received. "In fact when they first posted the 182," Stevens says, "I thought they had made a mistake and would quickly correct it and make it 282, but, of course, it didn't happen."

The following fifteen minutes at the convention were of high drama. To avoid pursuing reporters, Stevens gathered with his key organizers in a hockey dressing room underneath the stands at the Civic Centre — a meeting that turned out to be crucial to the convention. In the history of federal leadership conventions where backroom gatherings are commonplace, it is difficult to top this behind-the-scenes manoeuvre for the impact it had on the other candidates. Huddled in the room with Stevens were members of Parliament Bill Kempling, Bob Wenman, Peter Elzinga, Arnold Malone, Perrin Beatty, Bruce Halliday, Dean Whiteway, Howard Johnston and Albert Cadieu; Reg Stackhouse, a former MP; Don Hutchison, Stevens' floor manager at the convention; Dick Clewes, president of McKim Advertising; Don Blenkarn, the candidate's campaign manager; Ted Rowe, his riding campaign chairman; Trevor Jones, Stevens' official agent; Shirley Walker, his secretary; Stevens' wife, Noreen; Don McPhail, president of Comtech Group International Limited, and John Morand, treasurer of the same company.

Naturally the participants were despondent. "How did it happen?"

asked Bill Kempling. Blenkarn wondered aloud, "Where did our youth vote go?" However, the sombre mood was quickly broken as the clock continued to tick away. All candidates faced a fifteen-minute deadline after each ballot during which time they had to decide if they would be officially on the next ballot. By the time Stevens and his organizers assembled for their private meeting, eight minutes had passed.

It is not altogether clear how the decision to support Clark was made. Given the hectic atmosphere in the room at the time, it is not surprising that several of the participants remember it differently. What is evident is that when Stevens polled the group, a majority of them — perhaps as many as two-thirds — favoured Clark, with Wagner the second choice. Jones, the official agent, mentioned Horner. He said that there had been a tacit understanding with Stan Schumacher, Horner's official agent, that if Stevens came out on top, Horner's votes would swing to Stevens. Therefore, it seemed only right that, with the positions reversed, their support should go to Horner. This idea seems not to have had any takers.

The minutes ticked away. Jones was now anxious for a decision, as the withdrawal deadline was rapidly approaching. With two minutes to go, Stevens called for silence. He asked to see the results of the first ballot and the line-up of candidates. During those two minutes his eyes never left the sheet of paper in front of him as he measured each of the candidates and their positions carefully. Suddenly and decisively, Stevens turned to Jones, gave him the withdrawal form and said: "Deliver this to [Lincoln] Alexander. You guys are on your own, but I'm going with Joe Clark."

Jones took the withdrawal form and rushed out to the convention floor, handing it to Alexander in the nick of time. Shortly afterwards, Stevens went on national television and publicly announced his support for Clark.

When Stevens was forced to withdraw from the race, many of his supporters, caught up in the intensity of the moment, broke into tears. The candidate's band leader, whose musical group had been one of the noisiest in the lobbies of downtown hotels during the week, had tears streaming down his face as he switched into the Clark theme song. Someone had placed a yellow kerchief around his neck. While the Stevens camp came to grips with its loss the Clark campaign got new life. Clark came on television to describe Stevens as "a great parliamentarian" and said he was delighted to "have him with me."

There were two qualities in particular about Clark that Stevens admired: his tenacity and his sincerity. But perhaps more important was the consideration that Clark was a westerner and that he had youth on his side. "We run the criticism that we are an old fogey party," Stevens says, "that somehow we don't relate to today's generation. Clark's youth was a bridge between young people and relatively old people and appointing Clark as leader made Trudeau the old man of the House."

In the interests of party unity, Stevens' decision to move to Clark has to be viewed as a master stroke. First, he effectively diluted the leftist aura around Clark, which had been reinforced in part by Flora MacDonald's move to him. Stevens, who was aligned with the rightists in the party, showed he was prepared to work with Clark. Secondly, his manoeuvre left Jack Horner with virtually no choice but to eventually opt for Wagner, thus showing the country that the quintessential right-wing prairie Conservative could link up with a Quebecker. Thirdly, Stevens bridged generations within the party and showed that a Bay Street financier could find harmony with a young westerner thirteen years his junior. Here was youth and the Establishment together in the Tory party at last.

Soon after Stevens had made his move to Clark, Jim Gillies, Heward Grafftey and John Fraser joined the Clark campaign. Fraser, in particular, had been influenced by Stevens' decision. In fact, Fraser had made up his mind to stay on for one more ballot. But after he learned of Stevens' choice he decided not to wait any longer and he too went to Clark.

While Stevens' move to Clark seemed to surprise many people, Lowell Murray, who had been associated with Clark from the early sixties in federal election campaigns, saw it as a natural shift. Clark had spoken to Murray early in the leadership campaign and expressed disappointment at losing supporters to Stevens. Stevens had read Clark accurately. He is a tenacious individual. "They should have been with me," he told Murray, "but they went to Stevens because I didn't get to them fast enough, but I'm going after them for secondary support." Murray then saw the Stevens decision somewhat differently. "I wasn't surprised at all the way things developed," he says. "Clark had more potential to grow on subsequent ballots than any candidate." Stevens estimates that something like 70 per cent of his 182 supporters followed him to Clark. On the second ballot, Clark leapt to 532, almost doubling his votes. Now he had momentum and looked like a winner. Nine hundred and sixty-nine on the third. Victory on the fourth.

The moment is his. The Conservatives have chosen a new leader — the youngest federal party leader in Canadian history.

But it was victory with a question mark. The schisms within the party were apparent before the watchful eye of the television camera. Clark had captured the leadership by a scant 65 votes. His first task was obvious, namely, to pull together a caucus, the majority of whose members had opposed his candidacy. Clark relied to some extent on Graham Scott, a former executive assistant to Robert Stanfield, to help him through those difficult first weeks before his own staff could be selected.

Even for the newly chosen leader, the aftermath of a political convention is anticlimatic and far removed from the hoopla and waving placards which preceded his crowning. Joe Clark was learning early the loneliness of high places. John Laschinger, the former national director of the party, remembers those hours immediately after Clark's win, the time when delegates are returning to their homes across Canada to assume regular responsibilities once again.

Laschinger talked to Graham Scott about noon hour the next day, learning in the conversation that Clark had no one with him. "I'm sitting here trying to make appointments for him," Scott said, "and trying to get people to see him."

Laschinger asked, "Where did all his supporters and workers go?"

Scott replied: "They all went home. They got the last plane out last night."

"You've got to be kidding," said Laschinger; "they got him elected and they left him here!"

A Political Manager is Born

If we can believe the behavioural scientists, early experiences clearly affect the perceptions of our politicians and statesmen and hence the quality of their leadership. In Joe Clark's case, High River, Alberta, about thirty miles south of Calgary, is where his roots are. He was born in that small farming community of a few thousand people on 5 June 1939, only four years after William Aberhart had led the Social Credit party to power in the province, making great use of radio in the process. Bible Bill, "the Rudy Vallee of Canadian politics," would croon his radio speeches out to the lonely countryside of Alberta, flavouring his religious messages with Social Credit propaganda. Later Clark, as a central organizer for Peter Lougheed, now the provincial Conservative leader, would help to bring thirty-odd years of Socred rule to an end. Yet throughout his formative years, Clark lived in a province of one-party politics. As he recalls it, "High River was a very Social Credit community then. Partisan politics was not a very dominant part of our life nor was it in Alberta."

The history of High River is typical of many prairie towns. At the end of the nineteenth century, the little community was in the doldrums. The railroad had failed to encourage the hoped-for settlers because the country was in the midst of a dry cycle. It was a cowtown, consisting of little more than a livery barn, a blacksmith shop, the big stone building of the High River Trading Company, the railway station, a Presbyterian church and a few dwellings. At this time, the prairies were virgin country but did not remain so for long. In the early 1920s with the drought broken, there was a great influx of settlers.

The weekly newspaper started by Joe Clark's grandfather in 1905. Charles Clark journeyed out West in 1903 upon discharge from Boer War service.

New communities have to be serviced with some form of news media and, in the midst of this "changing west," Joe Clark's grandfather founded the *High River Times*. Upon discharge from Boer War service, Charles Clark had arrived in the West in 1903. After dabbling in real estate and horse-buying in Calgary, he went back to his real love, which was the newspaper business. His brother, Hugh Clark, editor of the *Kincardine Review* in Ontario, had trained him in the business. So in 1905, Charles Clark established his *High River Times* in an old drugstore. Putting out a weekly was a tough business in those days, and men and machines worked long hours. The staff were a willing bunch of workers because, during those handsetting days, they would often toil until one or two in the morning to release the paper for outgoing mail.

23

Recalling Charles Clark's death in 1949 and his community contribution, the *Times*, while saluting Alberta's Golden Jubilee year in Confederation on 18 August 1955, pointed with pride to the newspaper and its generational continuity:

> His genial presence is still much missed by the staff of the Times office, and by the old friends who drop in to visit, and whom he used to welcome so warmly. His son, C.A. Clark, has succeeded him, and his endeavour is to pursue the principles of justice and kindliness on which the paper was founded. It is an encouraging evidence of family continuity that young Joe Clark has been contributing to the paper in special assignments during the past year.

The newspaper game held "young Joe's" interest only for a short span of years, his attention having focused on other pursuits at a relatively early stage in life.

During the first quarter of the twentieth century, High River grew slowly and, as it did, the *Times* circulation increased. But given the political climate in the province, publishing a weekly newspaper during the depression was a hazardous business, as Joe's father discovered. Only one or two of the sixty-five weeklies in Alberta supported the Social Credit government. The *High River Times* was on the side of the majority of newspapers which did not believe in and even feared the party's policies. The Aberhart government sought to control the press, recognizing that the weeklies were as important a channel of communication to the people as was radio, the newer medium. Charles Clark can remember being chased home from Socred meetings, because the *High River Times* was on the party's enemy list. "They tried to keep us out of meetings," he recalls, "unless we signed papers committing ourselves to Social Credit policies."

The household in which Joe grew up was politically ambidexterous. Charles, his father, was a Conservative and his mother a Liberal. "I voted for Mackenzie King when I was twenty-one," says Grace, "because at that time it was sacrilege not to." Yet the political life of High River was predominantly Social Credit. Followers of the old-line parties were clearly in the minority and, in light of this fact, Grace and her husband's sister, an active Conservative like Charles, used to joke that they were the only two of their breed in town.

Looking back on his High River days, the Conservative leader considers

Grace and Charles Clark, parents of the Conservative leader, at their home on 725 Macleod Trail where Joe grew up. His sense of history was nurtured in conversations with the pioneer settlers of High River. In his formative years the Social Credit party dominated the town's political life.

the perception of him as a serious youngster determined at an early age to become prime minister as overblown.

"There is a feeling that I started at age two," he says. "That, in my judgment, is just not true." He admits that he was clearly not cut out to be a rancher or a rodeo rider during high school days. "I think there were some people in town who were certain that I was going to go on and do something. But I think that has to be put into the context of the certainty that a number of other teachers in a number of other towns have about the future progress of somebody else who turns out to sell insurance."

At times, the memories of parents and friends seem to conflict. Yet there emerges the general picture of a serious youngster, mature for his years and fond of talking to older people; a determined, individualistic youth

Elevator row in High River.

given more to reading, debating and essay-writing than to athletics. His friend Jim Howie, now a fertilizer dealer in the town, describes him as "not that well co-ordinated physically" and a student "who was always trying to tie the teachers in knots with his big words." His parents maintain that, at one time, he had an ambition to be a sportswriter and sports broadcaster; he played a lot of baseball, because he was too small for hockey. They recall him memorizing the *Encyclopedia of Sports*.

Perhaps the most convincing portrayal of the real Joe Clark is in the female perceptions of two former high school cheerleaders, the same age. Jeanette Alwood Rousseau, who still lives in High River, was a member of the High River Teen Town and remembers the sock-hops, listening to Elvis Presley and the almost docile attitude of the teenagers. "As a group our class seemed to be unusual in that we didn't tear around and drink," she says, "Joe was more interested in politics than the usual teenage scene." Recalling those days when the group would gather at the New Look Café for pop, she says Joe would occasionally come but not regularly. "Early in his teens he was really interested in politics," she says, "he seemed to know where he was going at 15 or 16."

Then there are the recollections of Penny Forsyth Wallace, one of the few girls Clark dated in High River during high school days. Now living in Silver Springs in north Calgary, she first met him in grade nine when she was 14, her family having just moved to High River. She and Jeanette were close friends and both popular students. Her memories of the few times Clark dated her invariably come back to the same theme. He had his life well charted at about age 16; politics was foremost on his mind. Their dates took them to drive-ins and local restaurants. But most of the time they would drive around High River, Joe having just obtained his driver's licence, and discuss the current political scene.

"We would argue constantly about politics," she says. "He talked a lot about an uncle who was in politics." (Colonel Hugh Clark sat for ten years in Parliament as the member for Bruce County, Ontario-Kincardine. In his speech to the party's leadership convention prior to voting, Clark reminded the delegates that he was the second of his family to have served in the House of Commons. "He was here the night the Parliament Buildings burned — and said the best place to watch that fire was from the balcony of the Rideau club, where he stood with other Conservative MPs from Ontario, who all watched with particular keenness the door to the Senate, to see which Senators didn't escape, and consequently what vacancies might be created.")

Clark's interest in debating, if not in the art of politics itself, was nurtured by a somewhat unlikely source, the High River Rotary Club. (On 23 April 1977 the Conservative leader could stand before the Rotary International in Niagara Falls, Ontario, and remind Rotarians they were to blame for his ending up in the savage world of politics.)

In 1956 Clark, at the age of 17, managed to win a Rotary scholarship after entering the Rotary and Oddfellow public speaking competition. The prize was a trip to Ottawa, where the raucous pipeline debate was in full swing. The legendary C.D. Howe and the then prime minister Louis St. Laurent had reached an agreement with representatives of Ontario, Alberta and a new commercial company, Trans-Canada Pipe Lines, on 1 September 1955. The pact spelled out the financial terms whereby natural gas would be transmitted from the Alberta fields to the markets of eastern Canada. However, from the opposition standpoint, the disquieting aspect to the agreement was the heavy dependence upon American capital. Historian Donald Creighton captured the essence of the Canadian dilemma. "Though Trans-Canada Pipe Lines had been formed, under federal government pressure, by the union of two companies, one substantially Canadian-owned and the other an American subsidiary, the controlling interest in the joint organization lay securely in the hands of American capitalists." Moreover, the company which was to supply most of the natural gas was also American-controlled. The project had another dubious side: while one of the markets which Trans-Canada Pipe Lines hoped to exploit was the urban centres of Ontario and Quebec, the other was located south of the boundary in the state of Minnesota. Naturally, the opposition in Parliament was disturbed at the terms of the agreement and through May and June 1956 the debate dragged on.

But the debate over Bill C-298 took on added significance for Parliament when Howe, the Liberal trade minister, introduced the initial resolution stage of the bill. Before the debate had begun, the impetuous minister served notice that the government would impose closure, which strictly curtailed the time allocated for debate. Closure, a device to force a speedy vote, clearly smacked of arrogance, and the opposition, led largely by John Diefenbaker, portrayed the aging St. Laurent government as a tired regime drunk with power.

During his first visit to the nation's capital, Clark not only witnessed the historic debate and closure but also met Conservative leader George Drew and Diefenbaker, Drew's successor. Indeed, it was the pipeline debate which served as a springboard for Diefenbaker to capture the Conservative leadership, a prize that had eluded him twice before. The trip to Ottawa stimulated a new political enthusiasm in Clark, who now claims that it was then that "his interest in politics became articulate." He returned to High River after watching the debate and Grace recalls her son believing that "we don't have democracy in this country. It's run by one party, and it should have an effective and strong opposition."

In the following year Clark was the student president at High River high school when Diefenbaker spoke there during the election campaign of that year. It was a moment of inspiration for the youthful Clark and subsequently he would turn down three other possible careers (law, teaching and journalism) in favour of politics.

From the year in which he travelled to Ottawa on that Rotary scholarship, Clark seems to have hardly looked back. While he flirted with several careers and attended a number of institutions of higher learning in Canada, politics was paramount in his life. It could be said that he never let his studies interfere with his political education. Soon after he entered the University of Alberta in the fall of 1957, Clark became active in the campus Tory club. But he also spent as much as forty hours a week working as a reporter on the *Gateway*, the student newspaper, which was published twice a week. Periodically he would startle the university administration with his satirical pieces on the Social Credit government in Alberta. On one occasion, the university confiscated most of the copies of the newspaper after Clark had sharply parodied Premier Ernest Manning. Clark spent his summers at this time working as a reporter for the *Edmonton Journal* and the Canadian Press in Calgary. In 1959 Clark served as private secretary to the Alberta Conservative leader, W.J.C. Kirby, who was then involved in a provincial election campaign.

After graduating from the University of Alberta in 1960 with a BA in history, Clark left for Europe and France where he wanted to improve his French. He was back in Canada the following year working at Conservative national headquarters in Ottawa writing party literature for the 1962 federal campaign. Here he met Lowell Murray, then executive assistant to Davie Fulton, justice minister in the Diefenbaker government. It was the beginning of a lengthy and close friendship as the two young men worked together in federal election campaigns throughout the 1960s, organizing party policy conferences and enjoying holidays together.

Clark appears to have been heavily influenced by his first real introduction to election campaigns at the federal level. The 1962 campaign, generally recognized as this country's first scientific election, saw opinion polls, surveys and political strategy reach a new high in sophistication. At the time, Clark worked for Allister Grosart, then the national director of the party, and a former advertising executive skilled in new organizational methods and campaign techniques. Grosart was the idea man behind the party's successful campaigns in 1957-58 and author of the famous Diefenbaker call sign, "My Fellow Canadians."

Political parties were undergoing significant changes in the late fifties and early sixties. The party process was slowly being de-politicized; a new breed of political managers entered Liberal and Conservative ranks replacing the older party advisers. On the Liberal side, Richard O'Hagan, Keith Davey and Tom Kent were representative of this fresh approach and their counterparts in the Conservative party, Grosart and Dalton Camp, also typified this managerial change. Increasingly, political leaders were turning to true professionals and specialists for advice. Clark seems to have been fascinated by this revolution. Whenever there was a federal campaign, a Tory annual meeting or an intra-party struggle, Clark was a backstage presence. During these years, he focused heavily on the political process, learning the intricacies of policy formulation, campaigning and party organization. In short, he was honing his skills as a political manager in the back rooms of the Conservative party.

In the early 1960s Clark also showed a keen interest in discovering how federal policies formulated in Ottawa affected the various regions of the country. Lowell Murray remembers Clark's interest in trying to learn more about Canada's distinctive features. Clark enrolled in the Dalhousie Law School in Halifax, but Murray viewed it as a move to help him understand the country rather than a true desire to study law. "He wanted an excuse to spend a year in the Maritime provinces," Murray says, "and find out what made the place tick. The next time I saw him after the 1962 campaign was in Halifax and after that he went out to the University of British Columbia. The consuming interest in his life was to find out what made the regions and people tick."

Whatever his motive, Clark admits that, as a student, the subject of law was a giant bore to him and so he dropped it. One of his favourite expressions used to be, "I wanted to become a lawyer until I met one." To this day, he is unsure as to whether the practice of law would have been challenging enough for him and frankly asserts that, even as a student, he backed into the field. It was in fact a Jimmy Stewart movie that aroused his curiosity about the profession. He remembers that in the film, "Anatomy of a Murder," Stewart did a lot of fishing. "I thought that was fine," says Clark with a slight grin, "and for that reason I enrolled in law."

From 1962 to 1965 Clark served as national president of the Progressive Conservative Students Federation. As its president he was chosen to introduce John Diefenbaker at a crucial session of the Conservative party's annual meeting in Ottawa from 1 to 5 February 1964. The national presidency of the Students Federation was a sensitive position in the mid-1960s as the anti-Diefenbaker movement grew within the party. In the third volume of his memoirs, *The Tumultuous Years*, Diefenbaker outlined some of the developments within the party prior to the important annual meeting. "I found it difficult to take seriously reports I received in January 1964," he wrote, "that those who opposed me were engaged in attempting to convince the rank and file that I had stifled both freedom of expression and the forward march of our party. This from people the majority of whom could not get themselves elected to any public office."

On the afternoon of 4 February Clark, who was 23 years old at the time, rose to praise Diefenbaker for the poise he had shown while under fire. In his speech to the annual meeting, Clark said that the question of Diefenbaker's leadership was a cause of discord within the party and the former prime minister had chosen to let the annual convention decide on that issue. "It was the choice of a great and strong man," he said. Clark told the convention that he had become a Conservative in 1956 because of Diefenbaker's stirring leadership. Before that, the party "did not reach out to me or to the country." Speaking directly to the party leader, Clark said, "You changed the course of government to meet the demands of a modern world."

It was a speech that endeared Clark to many party supporters. "He made a gangbuster of an introduction to Dief at a time when Dief's enemies in the party outnumbered his friends," Dalton Camp remembers. "The whole thing was that the young people were not going for Dief and Joe really did a masterful job."

Bridging generations. Former prime minister John Diefenbaker and Clark are shown attending the Remembrance Day service on 11 November 1976, four days before the Parti Québecois victory in Quebec.

Despite the pre-convention mutterings about discontent and disillusion with Diefenbaker's leadership, when it came to the crunch that afternoon, there was no public criticism of the leader by any of the delegates, and there was no official call for a leadership convention at that time.

Somewhat ironically, Clark later found himself having to oppose Diefenbaker, a leader he had once greatly admired. Forty-odd years separated the pair and Clark, as the students' representative, eventually had to admit publicly that the positions taken by Diefenbaker were "often out of step with the aspirations of younger Canadians." He singled out Diefenbaker's policy on the flag and national unity as two of the most offensive stands in the eyes of young party members. However, Clark also tried to play down the opposition to Diefenbaker as it related to personalities in the party. As he still maintains today, Clark said at the time of the upheaval within Conservative ranks that he firmly believed party disagreements should be made in private.

The ferment of change sweeping Canadian politics in the mid-1960s was also reflected on university campuses; students were questioning the validity of such established institutions as Parliament, big business and the church. As a lecturer in political science at the University of Alberta from 1965 to 1967, Clark found himself in the midst of the post-Beatle generation which was more preoccupied with sex and drugs than traditional learning.

"What bothered me about university teaching," he says, "was that I could never separate the teaching function out from the relationship with students. I was one to whom all students came with their personal problems, and that bothered me for two reasons. The lesser reason was that I was not professionally trained to deal with the range of social problems that were arising in Canadian universities." Secondly, it was not that he felt consultation with students was necessarily a waste of time. Rather he experienced frustration in not being able to help them. "I was alarmed by the number of students who didn't take an interest in the course," he said. "I kept feeling there were people in my class who were there for other reasons than to learn about political science."

While he was responsible for teaching about one hundred and fifty students, Clark's daily activity was not confined to the classroom. Again, politics remained his number one interest and teaching now paralleled his political pursuits, just as the study of law had done earlier. Clark would spend generally three days away from the university preparing provincial Conservatives for the forthcoming election campaign against the long-established Social Credit government. Indeed, while at the university he regarded himself as "more of a politician in residence than a lecturer." Twenty-seven years old at the time, Clark claimed that "people can't do anything well unless they are wrapped up in it." Clearly politics was to be the overriding passion in his life.

The organizational talent Clark had developed since his first interest in politics during the late 1950s manifested itself in the 1967 provincial election campaign. A year earlier, he had become director of the Conservative party's provincial organization and the driving force behind Peter Lougheed's campaign to defeat the Socreds. Stressing that the Conservative party could not wait for the people to come to it, Clark worked strenuous, eighteen-hour days on constituency organization and preparing party policy. He urged the party to adopt a more positive tone in its campaigning. In previous provincial campaigns the Conservatives had rather negatively concentrated on attacking the Social Credit government record. Clark emphasized the need for Peter Lougheed, who represented a new generation in western Canada, to outline clearly his goals and objectives for the province and thus focus voter attention on the Conservative platform. This new style of campaign, much the same as Clark's drive for the federal leadership a decade later, contrasted sharply with the traditional approach taken by the Socreds. The party in power still relied on billboards and political patronage, while the Conservatives methodically conducted a well-organized door-to-door campaign.

Clark, seeking public office himself for the first time in the riding of Calgary-Millican, then occupied by the Speaker of the provincial House, Art Dixon, was defeated. But the Conservative party, with six out of a total of sixty-five seats, became the official opposition in the Alberta legislature. The party's breakthrough in 1967, for which Clark was largely responsible, actually was the prelude to its smashing victory in the province four years later, which broke the Socreds' thirty-six-year reign.

With the provincial party in Alberta greatly strengthened, Clark again turned his attention to the federal level, where his true interest always lay. The party's 1967 federal leadership convention was only a few months away and Clark joined his long-time friend Lowell Murray, who was managing Davie Fulton's campaign. Also working for Fulton was Brian Mulroney, another strong organizer. This trio had reassessed the party's position in the province of Quebec and realized that, with the changing mood in the province, new strategies would have to be adopted.

"Unlike most of the other Conservatives," wrote Peter Newman in *The Distemper of Our Times*, "they realized it was no longer possible for political bosses to deliver the Quebec vote. It remained desirable to recruit the influential Montreal power-broker lawyers, but now their mandate had been reduced, with most delegates making up their own minds and ignoring the dictates of the once-powerful political overlords. The best way to capture the Quebec vote was to stump the province, riding by dusty riding, and this was what Fulton proceeded to do."

Clark's organizing skills on behalf of Fulton greatly impressed the eventual winner of the leadership convention, Robert Stanfield, who hired him as his speech-writer and executive assistant. Clark and Murray (who had become Stanfield's first chief of staff), again teamed up together in the office of the leader of the opposition. As it turned out, the move for Clark was an

Joe Clark and Davie Fulton, former federal justice minister in the Diefenbaker government at a Vancouver Canadian Club reception in January 1977. Clark was a central organizer in Fulton's unsuccessful campaign for the party leadership in 1967.

Lowell Murray, a long-time friend of the Conservative leader and his election campaign chairman. Murray's pensive mood was captured on 24 May 1977, the night six federal by-elections were lost by the Tories.

ideal training ground for the job he would occupy nine years later. Watching the process from the inside provided him with a further opportunity to determine where the organization of the leader's office and federal wing of the party could be improved.

In 1970 Clark left the leader's office to tour Europe and to resume French studies, returning to Canada year later to finish his Master of Arts in political science, which he obtained in 1973. His thesis was entitled "Policy Conferences of Major Parties in Canada as Innovating Agencies." In considering the work as an insight into Clark's political philosophy, it must be remembered that theses always are written for supervisors and examining boards. Any conclusions to be drawn about his approach to politics must take these inherent constraints into account. Nevertheless, the thesis seems to mirror Clark's political career in that up to the time it was written his experience had been in the party backrooms and on the managerial side of politics. In general, the thesis is more the thinking of the political manager than it is of the party politician. Clark does not appear to be a genuine party man.

"Nobody much likes major parties," he writes, "they are put up with, like work or weather, but most people wouldn't want their daughter to join one." Moreover, he feels that parties and their leaders should not rely solely on their caucuses for advice. "Parties would wither if they listened only to their parliamentary caucus or the loyal constellations around caucus." He concludes that "however important to the public at large, it is of critical importance to the members of the party to witness a demonstration of a wider range of party talents than is evident in Parliament."

On the same theme, Clark maintains that opposition parties cannot rely solely on their performances in Parliament to win office. "An inept performance in official opposition," he writes, "might prejudice a party seeking to mount a successful campaign outside Parliament, but there is little evidence to suggest that the effective performance of the role of official opposition has had any more than a marginal influence in campaigns which succeeded in changing governments."

During his first successful campaign as a political candidate Clark, as would be expected, relied heavily on organization and management to win office. In 1971 he decided to seek the party nomination in the Alberta riding of Rocky Mountain. In a sense, Clark was looked upon as an outsider, because his home community of High River lay just beyond the boundaries of the federal seat, which was held by Liberal Allan Sulatychy. Because of its size, nominating conventions were held in ten centres throughout the huge riding of thirty-four thousand square miles. At the final meeting held in Drayton Valley, where Clark won the nomination, he called for a more positive approach to politics, particularly in the West. "The West has been so busy complaining it can't reach a positive conclusion. The future of Canada is not in Toronto or Montreal — it's out here on the building end of Canada." Describing Sulatychy, who was parliamentary secretary to the then northern affairs minister Jean Chretien, as "a popular man representing an unpopular party," Clark was determined "to drive home Liberal unpopularity and create as strong a personal appeal as Allan."

The strategy paid off. In the election of 30 October 1972 Clark received some five thousand votes more than Sulatychy. He credited his win to the anti-Trudeau feeling in the country "and a low profile top organization." However, it had been a tough campaign and not without rancour. Sulatychy's campaign manager, Kelly Loder, charged that the *Edmonton Journal* had helped make Clark the winner by an unfair press — "the worst to us in all Alberta" — and said "the people got what they deserved, a man that isn't even from the riding." Loder blamed his candidate's defeat on the Trudeau backlash. John Wise, a freshman MP from Ontario, saw from the start that Clark was a more able parliamentarian than a number of other MPs elected for the first time in 1972. Wise remembers how the member from Rocky Mountain stood out from other newcomers. "I was impressed by his ability to grasp the feeling of the House of Commons."

The Leader's Team

After the leadership convention, Joe Clark moved rapidly to put his individual stamp on the party. The changes he made reflected the difference between his style of leadership and that of his predecessor Robert Stanfield. After eleven years as premier of Nova Scotia, Stanfield had been 53 years old when he became opposition leader. He had brought old times to the office and relied on such tough political veterans as Finlay MacDonald, the hard-drinking Cape Breton businessman who eventually became his chief of staff. But Stanfield had seemed unable to grasp the true meaning of the communications revolution sweeping through Canadian politics in the fifties and sixties. Politicians now had to be capable television performers to gain power. The campaign era when the party message was shouted to the back of the hall had ended.

For Stanfield, this transition was a difficult one. Moreover, like other provincial premiers who had tried it, he found the shift from provincial politics to the federal arena was a quantum leap. "You walk out and they shove a bunch of microphones in your face," he once said, "and in 30 seconds you're expected to produce a profound and intelligent answer...to an extremely complicated national issue." Indeed, Stanfield tended to see most national issues in terms of his home province, and, despite his sound knowledge of economics and world affairs, lacked an understanding of the subtle differences among the various regions in Canda. Lowell Murray, Stanfield's first chief of staff in Ottawa, at times was surprised how regularly Nova Scotia served as the Conservative leader's vantage point. "He used to make these Nova Scotia jokes about Toronto," Murray remembers,"not realizing that they didn't go over at all and you just don't do that sort of thing."

When Stanfield became leader in 1967, the operation of the leader's office resembled that of a country store and was virtually devoid of any semblance of technical organizational efficiency. Like opposition leaders before him, Stanfield had to contend with a meagre budget and small staff. Murray recalls the "tiny, tiny staff" of fifteen people around Stanfield in 1969. However, in that same year, Parliament made provision for a research office which took a heavy burden off the leader's staff and provided Stanfield with a wider range of policy material.

By contrast, Clark brought to the office a broader outlook. He knew the country better and also had a much closer relationship with party notables, given his lengthy political apprenticeship since the late 1950s.

He now has an office staff of forty people, almost three times the number his predecessor had in the beginning, and comparable to Lester Pearson's staff when he was prime minister. Yet Clark's office, in the number of personnel, pales in comparison to the East Block where Pierre Trudeau's eighty-six office employees receive annual salaries totalling $1,551,196. The Conservative party, as official opposition, is allotted between $600,000 and $660,000 for thirty-six staff positions. The four extra positions in the leader's office are paid for by the party itself. The House of Commons allots the official opposition $294,000 for operation of its research office, which has assumed an increasingly important role since Clark became leader. Clark is probably deploying his talent and utilizing the resources available to him more effectively than any opposition leader before him. In actual fact, he is functioning more as the leader of a government in waiting than simply as the leader of a critical opposition.

With more resources at his disposal, Clark has been able to streamline the organization of his office and introduce to it his special managerial style. Whereas most previous leaders have relied for advice on a handful of party stalwarts, with close access to them, Clark has espoused a form of leadership which stresses group decision-making. Clearly, a striking characteristic of the office Joe Clark manages is the emphasis on group, instead of individual, action.

Politicians in the 1960s frequently borrowed management ideas from the business community, the kind of management John Kenneth Galbraith discusses in his book *The New Industrial State*. Clark gained his best political experience throughout the sixties and he could hardly be expected to overlook these new methods.

> The modern business organization, [Galbraith writes], or that part which has to do with guidance and direction, consists of numerous individuals who are engaged, at any given time, in obtaining, digesting or exchanging and testing information. The most typical procedure is through the committee and the committee meeting. One can do worse than think of a business organization as a hierarchy of committees. Coordination, in turn, consists in assigning the appropriate talent to committees, intervening on occasion to force a decision, and, as the case may be, announcing the decision or carrying it as information for a yet further decision by a yet higher committee.

As leader, Clark has formed teams and committees which seem to be everywhere throughout the party. Besides his own personal team in the leader's office, there is a special leader's committee on organization chaired by Clark's close friend Harvie Andre, the member for Calgary Centre; a strategy committee which includes an inner circle of caucus members, serves as a sounding board for Clark mainly on long-range party matter; and a policy advisory council under the chairmanship of Reva Gerstein, a Toronto psychologist and business executive, is charged with the responsiblity of recommending a wide range of policies. This council, which includes Toronto's Mayor David Crombie among its members, reports directly to Clark and not to the caucus or the party. These various structures combine caucus members, non-elected party members and recognized experts in team decision-making, thus providing Clark with balanced recommendations and criteria to draw upon before he personally reaches a final decision. As he told a Conservative fund-raising dinner in May 1976, the party must "hear and heed contributions from all sources."

It is the leader's office, however, that remains the nerve centre of the party on a day-to-day basis. Clark has assembled around him a group of loyalists whose vision of the world is focused on the East Block on Parliament Hill. They are young professionals who were in a buoyant mood during their first year with Clark as Gallup polls were repeatedly favourable to the party. After the Parti Québecois victory of 15 November 1976 and a sudden resurgence in Liberal support, their enthusiasm waned somewhat;

Bill Neville, Clark's chief of staff.

Bill Neville, Clark's chief of staff.

but they are still convinced that Clark is on the threshold of becoming the next prime minister of Canada.

Clearly, Clark's staff have their own personal ambitions; they aspire to the Prime Minister's Office — they are not the kind to be associated with lost causes. They are not party people in the traditional sense. Rather, they have experience and expertise to sell and are inclined to view the Conservative party more as a client than solely as a political instrument.

Bill Neville, Clark's chief of staff, is one of the more experienced members of the office and the leader's principal adviser. From 1968 to 1974 he was executive vice-president of Lee-Neville Executive Consultants which he formed with Bill Lee, a former executive assistant to Paul Hellyer. Essentially, Neville and Lee advised large corporations on what was transpiring in Ottawa and whom to talk to in the nation's capital. They also provided names for cabinet members who might be looking for executive assistants. Indeed, Neville has a thorough knowledge of Ottawa, the workings of Parliament and the Conservative party itself, having at one time been director of the party's research office.

His advice to Clark ranges from suggestions on how the leader's time can be best spent to matters of policy and caucus considerations. In large

Ian Green, Clark's executive assistant.

measure, Neville decides who the leader will see and when he'll see them. As chief of staff, he looks for efficiency and a steady pace in the office. He remains determined to get rid of the Grits, the party he once worked for as executive assistant to Judy LaMarsh. He is also tough. "There are times when somebody has to say no, whether it's to a request or whatever. I'd much sooner it be said by a staff person and the guy goes away mad but thinking, Christ, Clark's a nice guy, it's those bastards that work for him."

Until September 1977, when he was promoted to executive assistant, Clark's legislative assistant was Ian Green, whose quick wit at times provided a touch of relief amidst the intensity of the working day. A former executive assistant to the national party president Michael Meighen, Green

42

Above right: Patrick Howe, Clark's legislative assistant. Above: Donald Doyle, Clark's press secretary.

has been the leader's assistant and contact point on legislative matters. He was also responsible for liaison between the leader's office and caucus. In this latter role, it has been his task to strive for a good working relationship with caucus members and to ease the inevitable tension that rises between the leader's staff and the parliamentary caucus. Green worked for the Tories in the 1972 and 1974 election campaigns and was secretary to the leadership convention committee.

Donald Doyle, the leader's press secretary, is a former parliamentary correspondent for *Le Soleil*. His contacts with the French media in Quebec are invaluable to Clark, who is trying to strengthen the party's organization in that province. Doyle, who is bilingual, sits in on French media interviews;

if Clark is stuck for a word in French, he will turn to his press secretary for assistance. Doyle says he never realized how important time was until he took the job as press secretary. "When you are a journalist you think only of one deadline but in this job you have to think in terms of five, ten and fifteen minute blocks."

In September 1977 there was a realignment of duties in the office, aimed at getting still more efficiency into Clark's working day. Ian Green was made executive assistant to the leader, replacing Claude Boisselle, and a newcomer, Patrick Howe, joined the staff as Clark's legislative assistant. Howe has a background in journalism, having been on the staff of the *Globe and Mail* and served for brief periods in the CBC and with a London, Ontario, radio station.

On 1 October Duncan Edmonds joined the office as senior policy adviser, replacing Jim Hawkes who returned to the University of Calgary with the intention of seeking the party nomination in the new riding of Calgary West. The arrival of Edmonds in particular has given Clark's office greater depth. In the early 1960s Edmonds served on Lester Pearson's staff when the late prime minister was leader of the opposition. When Pearson retired in 1968, Edmonds directed Paul Martin's unsuccessful leadership campaign. Edmonds' appointment was hailed as major coup; Clark now had a senior policy adviser who could strengthen his links with the business community. This highly influential group seemed reluctant to consider Clark seriously as a future prime minister and one of Edmonds' functions was to give the Conservative leader more credibility in his dealings with the private sector. Moreover, it was a timely appointment, coming as it did just a month before the party's biennial policy convention in Quebec City. Clark's staff had been under attack from some caucus members and party workers for failing to project their leader in a more positive fashion.

Individually the members of Clark's staff are able people, but coordination between the Stanfield hold-overs and the newcomers has been a problem. For the first eighteen months or so, the new members seemed somewhat erratic and disorganized. Immediately after the leadership convention there was a period of what Edmonds describes as an "unrealistic escalation of support" to be followed by a "terrific tumble" in the wake of the election of the Parti Québecois. During this latter period, Clark's staff became demoralized and promoted activities that, on reflection, seemed ill-advised. "The tour that Clark took out to the west coast last spring," says

Duncan Edmonds, Clark's chief policy adviser. His task is to provide Clark with a coherent package of policy alternatives for the election campaign. Like Bill Neville, Edmonds is a former Liberal.

Edmonds, "he would have been better off if he had just stayed in bed."

Edmonds has brought a pragmatism and a sense of restraint to the leader's office. "I often advise doing less than doing more. We shouldn't get into a frantic hassle about this and that." Like Clark, Edmonds feels the official opposition should try to show initiative and not merely appear to be reacting to what the government says and does. One of Edmonds' first tasks in 1978 was to organize a conference on small business for the party. He also wants to increase the amount of time Clark spends outside the ranks of the Conservative party itself. "There is a wide section of voters out there that are not part of the party," he says; "you have to reach out to them also."

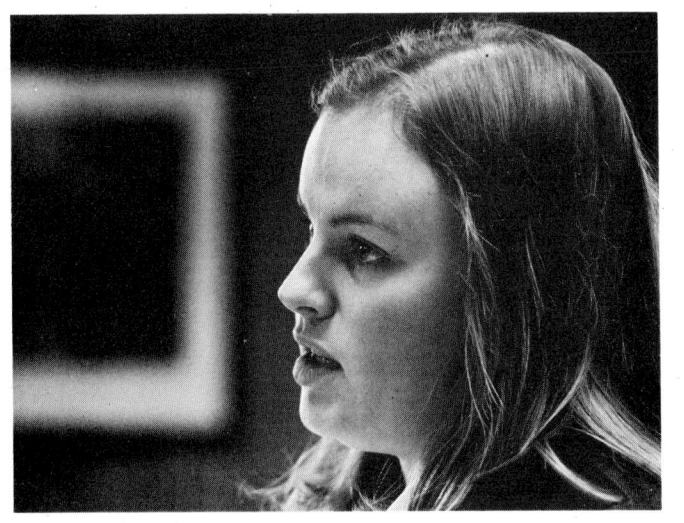

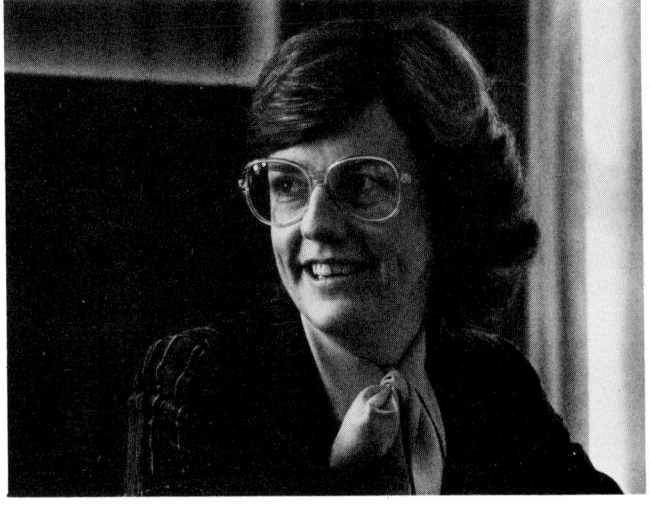

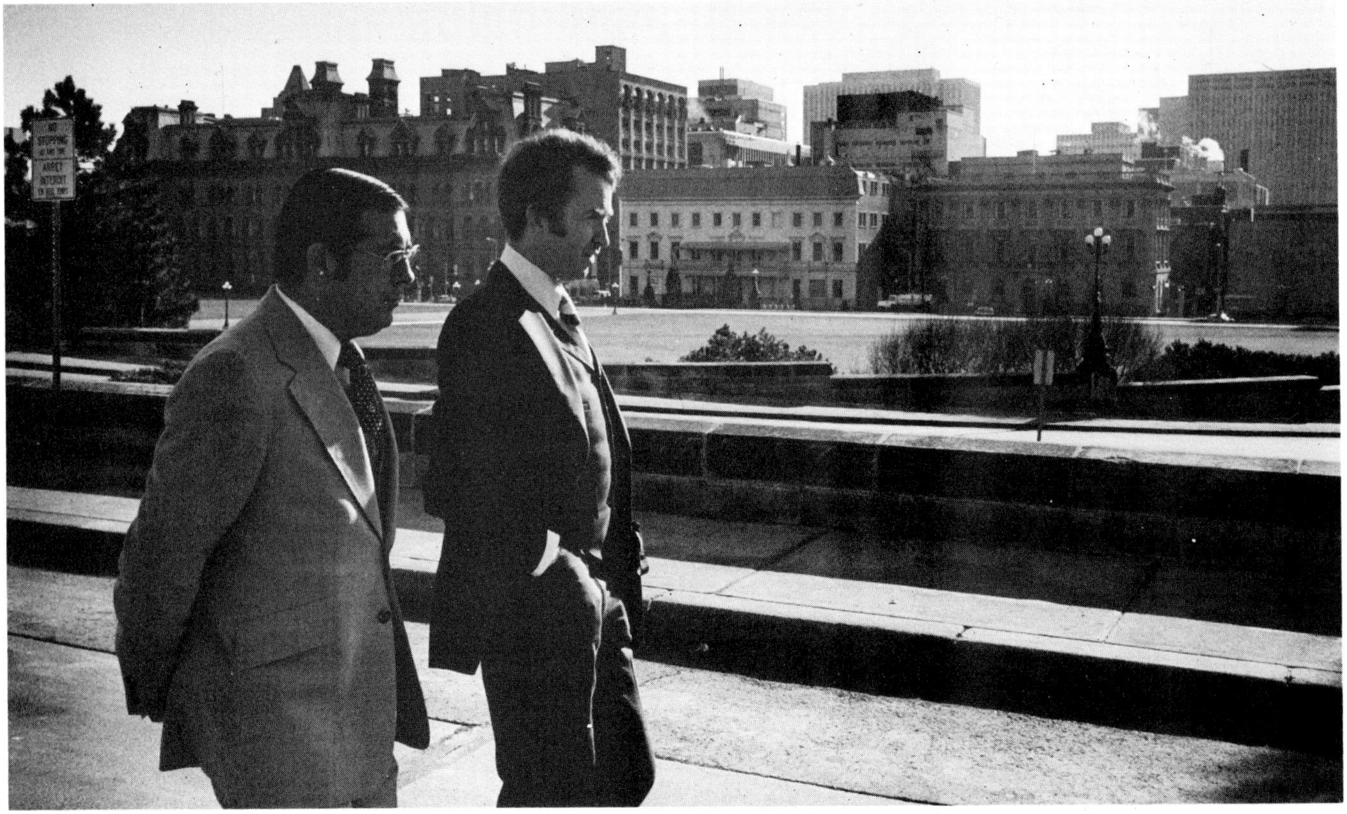
NO
STOPPING
ARRET
INTERDIT

Top right: *Jodi White, Clark's director of communications.* Top left: *Wendy Orr, the leader's appointments secretary.* Bottom: *Neville and Clark on their way to the West Block.*

Jodi White is one of a number of women among Clark's senior advisers. She is director of communications, a post created by Clark because he saw a need for the party to communicate more effectively with its followers outside of Ottawa. A former network radio producer for the CBC, White was involved in a number of current affairs programs such as "Capital Report." She is responsible for party mailing lists and keeping up contact with regional organizers. "When we started looking at things," she says, "we discovered that the mailing list for the national party was 30,000 people, which is just preposterous for a party trying to let people know what is happening." By the end of 1977 a new computerized mailing list had been compiled containing 110,000 names.

When White became director of communications, she soon saw that the party material had to be made more attractive. "The party documents looked like high school newspapers; they weren't part of this century in terms of what people are doing in the communications business." The party has since hired a graphics artist at national headquarters to give their promotional material a more professional look.

Since Clark took over the party leadership there has been more emphasis on integration of the leader's office, party headquarters and the research office. Clark sees himself as the leader of a team and it is this aspect of his leadership which he wants to sell to the country. Whereas Robert Stanfield was a party politician primarily concerned with the workings of caucus and the shadow cabinet, Joe Clark has shifted the emphasis more toward organization. With greater financial resources and staff than Stanfield, he is projecting himself as a leader waiting to form a government with as much access to advice and expertise outside the party's parliamentary wing as he has inside the caucus. This departure from the reliance on party stalwarts is seen by Clark as a necessary step in preparing to govern. In the event that he becomes prime minister, Clark wants an inventory of capable people available to come to Ottawa with him, lest his party should find itself captive to the public service. His own team of experts would counter the mandarins who for decades have been in the service of the Liberal party. In short, Joe Clark has moved the Conservative party beyond the age of the shadow cabinet to that of the shadow Prime Minister's Office.

A Day at the Office

The office of the official leader of the opposition is one of the most impressive on Parliament Hill, not so much for its decor as for its tradition. The octagonal room had at one time been the office of the prime minister of the day. After the 1963 election John Diefenbaker, whose office is now across the hall, decided he wanted to stay where he was even though the Liberals formed the government. Lester Pearson, then the prime minister, moved into a suite of offices on the third floor where Pierre Trudeau is now.

One of the most striking features of the office is the mural painted at ceiling level around the room. The blue frieze depicts angels, cherubs, British insignia and a woman meting out justice. The *Ottawa Citizen*, in a story before Joe Clark finished his first year in office, claimed the painting was in existence by 1937, when Mackenzie King occupied the office. The newspaper referred to a memo dated 17 February 1937, written by King's private secretary to the Ministry of Public Works, asking for certain changes in the mural. According to the *Citizen*, "it seems the changes involved having Mr. King's beloved mother painted into the mural. And there she is. An angel's face is hers, and again it is she who holds the sword."

The office itself has an overwhelming ambiance of history. Besides King, Louis St. Laurent and John Diefenbaker have occupied it as prime ministers. From behind the leader's desk, an overpowering portrait of Sir John A. Macdonald glares down from above a fireplace which is never used. Slightly to the left of the fireplace is a bust of Sir Robert Borden which has just been cleaned. Beside the bust is a small door which King apparently had installed so that he could hide from unwelcome visitors. The door now leads into the office of Clark's private secretary, Adele Desjardins.

The office of the leader of the opposition in the Centre Block on Parliament Hill. At one time it served as the office of the prime minister of the day.

49

There is a picture of the governor general, Jules Leger, on one wall and to the right of the desk, from the east wall, George-Etienne Cartier stares straight ahead. Cartier, spokesman and leader of the French-speaking wing of Macdonald's party, was a man given more to political action than to theorizing and, like the present leader, a Catholic. The pine-panelled office also contains bookshelves which hold bound copies of Hansard.

A dictaphone, which Clark uses frequently on his arrival in the morning to dictate messages to staff personnel, sits on the upper left portion of the desk. Close by is a baseball autographed by team members of the 1976 Montreal Expos. A framed photo of his wife and daughter sits on a small cabinet to the left. In front of the desk is a coffee table, five chairs and, under the portrait of Cartier, a black sofa. Through the windows behind the desk, the Langevin Building (named after Sir Hector-Louis Langevin, a Father of Confederation), the exclusive Rideau Club and the American embassy can be seen on Wellington Street. When the powerful fluorescent lights are turned on, the room becomes an octagon of brilliance. Amidst these surroundings, steeped in tradition, the young Conservative leader begins the first round of major business, the daily House leaders' meeting.

In effect, the House leaders' gathering each morning is a general strategy session covering the day ahead. Clark sometimes remains seated behind the desk in his office during these sessions. At other times, he will move to the front of the desk and sit in one of the chairs around the small coffee table, sipping coffee as he discusses the upcoming day's activities with the meeting's participants. The caucus chairman, Elmer MacKay, and the opposition whip, Steve Paproski, generally are seated on the sofa in the room. Also attending the meetings are Walter Baker, the House leader; Ray Hnatyshyn, the oral question period coordinator and deputy House leader; Bill Neville, Clark's chief of staff; Ian Green, his executive assistant and occasionally Donald Doyle, Clark's press secretary. These meetings last anywhere from twenty minutes to half an hour depending on the time available. On any given day, they can touch on a variety of subjects, including recent media coverage, caucus dissension, the party's positions on particular issues, how to counteract government publicity and the approach to be taken in the afternoon Question Period.

It is Monday, 18 April 1977. It has been decided at the House leaders' meeting to focus that day's Question Period on the economy in light of recent Statistics Canada figures which showed the jobless rate in the country

Burly Steve Paproski, the party whip, was first elected to the Commons in 1968. An early backer of Clark in his leadership campaign, Paproski has tried to play down his earlier buffoon image, assuming a more constructive posture in opposition.

The House leaders' meeting which starts Clark's working day. In conference with Clark are Walter Baker, the party's House leader; Bill Neville; Ray Hnatyshyn, deputy House leader; and (seated behind Hyatyshyn) Steve Paproski, the party whip. Given the highly partisan nature of the strategy sessions, these meetings can produce a range of emotions from sarcasm to humour.

to be 8.1 per cent, the highest since the depression. Parliament was resuming after an eleven-day Easter recess and the opposition felt that the government was vulnerable on the economy. The Tories lined up four or five speakers who would pursue the issue from several standpoints. The prime minister would not be in the Commons this day — he was in Winnipeg to address the annual meeting of the Canadian Association of Broadcasters on the issue of national unity — the questions would be directed to the acting prime minister, Allan MacEachen.

Between 10 a.m. and the noon hour Green, aided by party researchers and appropriate caucus members, prepares for Clark a lead question followed by three supplementaries. The opposition leader generally goes with the thrust of Green's questions but frequently applies his own wording

A familiar pose.

instead of what is written for him. After lunch, the two spend a hectic half-hour making last-minute adjustments to the prepared questions.

At 1.30 p.m. Ray Hnatyshyn comes into Green's office, which is just down from the leader's. Green shows him the lead question for Clark which Hnatyshyn feels is too weak.

"I think you could be stronger on the deteriorating economic situation," he says, "there is a need for some preamble." Hnatyshyn wants Clark to come down harder on the recent federal budget. "As far as we are concerned, the budget is a non-event. What we've got is a stand pat, political budget." It is now 1.40 p.m. and a secretary shouts, "Ian, the leader wants you."

Clark is seated in a chair in front of his desk, his legs crossed. The verbal exchanges between the two are brisk and to the point. Time is running out. In approximately 15 minutes the bells in the Centre and West blocks will summon members to the Commons.

Green hands the questions to Clark who sits and ponders the content of each while his aide paces nervously in front of him smoking a cigarette. The first question reads:

> Could I ask the Minister if, in light of Canada's deteriorating economic situation, we can expect a statement on motions later today informing the House of the Prime Minister's intentions, in his speech tonight, concerning national economic management which remains a central element in the confederation debate?

Green explains why the question is focused in the way it is. After a quick reading, Clark says, "So you want me to tie it to the speech tonight?" Green responds, "Bill [Neville] says you can't let the government talk about national unity without talking about economic management."

Clark wants to know what the unemployment rate is in Prince Edward Island. Green tells him. Then Sinclair Stevens, the party's financial critic, enters the office.

"The thing that I thought was most startling about the figures," says Stevens, "was that only three thousand jobs were created in the five eastern provinces where unemployment is highest." In Stevens' view, the more Clark can show he is attempting to come up with solid alternatives to the economic problems, the better for the party.

Stevens urges him to try to appear more non-partisan on the issue.

Doyle along with Ray Hnatyshyn accompany Clark to the chamber, though of the Tory caucus in the Commons. Generally, Green or press secretary position in the opposition leader's gallery which gives him a bird's eye view the Speaker directly across the aisle from the prime minister. Green takes his enters the historic chamber and goes directly to his seat located to the left of stairways before arriving in the foyer of the House of Commons. Clark into the question." Green and Clark then leave the office and race down the minister is away making a significant address on national unity and then go

Clark listens and decides: "Okay, I think I'll say I understand the prime questions. It is now almost two o'clock.

out of work." Green again reminds the opposition leader of the intent of the

"This thing is far past the partisan stage," he says, "there's a million people

The leader's daily agenda is filled with meetings, interviews and appointments. Clark frequently glances at the time hoping to stay on schedule, and often turns to his aides asking, "What's next?"

Clark on the way to the Commons.
Donald Doyle, his press secretary,
is immediately behind him.

they seldom use the elevator. If there is a mode of transportation Joe Clark seems to dislike, it is the elevator. When a stairway is nearby, he invariably chooses it. Moreover, Clark is a prisoner of his schedule. He frequently has to meet delegations on his way to Question Period and the elevator simply proves unsuitable for a politician trying to maintain personal contact. For example, the following day he stopped on his way to the Commons to greet a group of students from the riding held by Newfoundland member Jack Marshall, before proceeding to the chamber. His speedy gait clearly gives the impression even to casual observers that Clark is a young man in a hurry, exhausting though it may be on his personal staff.

The Speaker of the House calls the Commons to order and the Question Period begins. Clark leads off. The thrust of his first question is the same, but the words bear little resemblance to those his aides prepared for him.

> My question is to the acting Prime Minister. Since it is clear that one of the causes of disunity in Canada is the fact that east of the Ottawa Valley only one province — Prince Edward Island, the smallest province — has less than double digit unemployment today. Can the acting Prime Minister tell us whether in the Prime Minister's speech in Winnipeg — modestly described as significant — the Prime Minister intends to indicate the new initiatives the Government of Canada intends to take to create new jobs for the more than one million Canadians who are out of work and to bring to national policy some sense of national economic direction which will address this serious source of disunity in the nation?

The opposition leader goes on to urge the government to refer the problem of unemployment to a Commons committee.

The daily Question Period in the Commons ends around three o'clock. Clark is generally in attendance during this hour unless he is out of town. Question Period is by far the best opportunity for the opposition to score political points by stiff cross-questioning of ministers on the workings of their departments. If effective in the Commons, Clark can be assured of television coverage on the national news; hence these daily encounters with the prime minister and the government that he heads are extremely important.

Clark might prefer to spend more time in the Commons but, as party leader, his other commitments are too onerous to allow lengthy attendance. Therefore, he generally limits himself to Question Period, returning to the

When not in the House or at meetings, a large portion of Clark's day is often spent on the telephone.

Commons only on important occasions such as non-confidence votes or when he is to deliver a major speech.

At three p.m., Clark's working day is normally half over. However, every hour during this first week after the Easter recess in mid April 1977 seemed unusually long. Lingering caucus dissention was having an adverse effect on his credibility as party leader. The situation had to be checked quickly.

For almost a month Jack Horner, the prairie Conservative from the Alberta riding of Crowfoot, had been flirting with the Liberals and threatening to leave the Tories. Moreover, he appeared to be negotiating his eventual departure mainly through the news media without informing the Conservative leader of his intentions. Despite the fact that Horner's policy positions frequently had the backing of a relatively small faction in the party's caucus, the member for Crowfoot was adept at attracting media attention. Horner claimed that Clark had treated him shabbily in not living up to a commitment to guarantee him renomination in the riding of Crowfoot. Redistribution was at the root of the problem. About two-thirds of the voters in the new Crowfoot riding are now in the Battle River riding of freshman MP Arthur Malone, whom Horner maintained was actively campaigning to take the nomination away from him. According to Clark, he had never promised to guarantee Horner the nomination.

Clark was now facing his second major test as party leader in dealing with a fractious caucus. Earlier he had backed away from a potentially divisive quarrel with maverick Tory Stan Schumacher over who had the best claim to the nomination in the new riding of Bow River. To some party followers, Clark's choice of Yellowhead, his second preference as a federal seat, appeared to be a retreat and the decision no doubt caused him some public embarrassment. Yet he had defused a growing intra-party struggle that could have been far more damaging in the long run.

In the event, Clark was acclaimed as the Conservative candidate in the western Alberta constituency of Yellowhead but Schumacher was later to lose the party nomination in Bow River to Gordon Taylor, a former minister of highways in the Social Credit government and a popular figure who stressed the importance of party unity in his campaign. Soon after his defeat, Schumacher would charge that Clark supporters were responsible for his loss and describe the nomination campaign as a "grudge match."

However, in April 1977 Horner had made Clark appear as the leader of a party out of control. Clark had no choice then but to take some form of decisive action. On Monday afternoon, Clark issued an ultimatum to Horner giving him 48 hours to make up his mind on whether to leave the Conservative party. His statement came after Alberta MPs failed to resolve the dispute between Horner and Malone. Horner, who had given his support to Claude Wagner in his attempt to stop Clark from winning the party's leadership convention just over a year ago, had said he would announce his decision on whether he would join the Liberals sometime after Easter. Now Clark was forcing the matter and demanding a decision by 10 a.m. Wednesday, when the party's caucus would hold their regular weekly meeting.

The fat now was truly in the fire. On Tuesday morning, the day after the prime minister's Winnipeg speech, Bill Neville briefed the senior office members of the latest caucus developments at their regular weekly meeting. These meetings, initiated by Neville when he took over as chief of staff, are to allow the office members to share information and subsequently coordinate various activities. Among those in attendance on this day were Jim Hawkes, then Clark's program director responsible for the coordination of policy; Jodi White, Clark's director of communications; Wendy Orr, his appointments secretary; Morag Orecheski, special assistant for Clark's Rocky Mountain constituency; Marjory LeBreton, Clark's special assistant for tours; and his then speech writer, Gordon Galbraith. With Clark obviously under fire, the facial expressions at the meeting were noticeably tense as the participants listened to Neville.

When the House leaders met on that same morning, Clark brought up the matter of the prime minister's speech. "We have to discuss whether we do anything about that speech last night. I wanted to say the networks were conned but Bill's [Neville] better judgment prevailed. What was remarkable about the speech was the little understanding of Western Canada it showed. It was badly written, badly staged and badly received."

Reviewing the content of the speech, the opposition leader notes that it contained a quote from Wallace Stegner, a western author that he has quoted a number of times. "They had the good judgment to take his name out," he says.

Since this is only the second day back after the Easter recess, Ray Hnatyshyn tells the meeting that the Question Period should again focus on the economy and unemployment. This time, he wants to concentrate on what is referred to as "the repriorization of government spending." In other words, the opposition will tell the government where it feels spending could be reduced and urge that the money from those expenditures be directed toward creating jobs.

One of the areas of expenditure considered at the meeting is Petro Canada, the petroleum company established by the Liberals during the minority government days when the New Democratic Party held the balance of power. In November 1976 Clark disclosed in an interview that a Progressive Conservative government would move to wind down Petro Canada. However, on this particular day, Bill Neville is uneasy about the strategy being planned.

Walter Baker, the House leader, thinks the repetition of the economy theme is appropriate. Hnatyshyn agrees, saying, "You've got to club the

The day that changed Canadian history. Here Clark rehearses a prepared statement for television on the evening of the Parti Québecois victory on 15 November 1976. Bill Neville and Jodi White look on.

media over the head to get your point across." Before the meeting concludes, Clark says he feels Jacques Lavoie "spends an inordinate amount of time with Grit members. We've got to stop that." Another day planned, the meeting breaks up.

The opposition leader, in addition to an appointment with Lavoie, has a newspaper interview and a session with MPs Sinclair Stevens and John Fraser in the morning to prepare for a dinner meeting that evening at the Chateau Laurier with Joe Morris, president of the Canadian Labour Congress, and other labour leaders.

This particular day was extremely hectic for Clark; he had a special caucus meeting scheduled for 3.30 following Question Period, and he had to return to the Commons for a vote on an opposition motion of non-con-

Clark and his aides are deep in thought as they discuss the leader's 15 November statement to the nation. From left to right are: Claude Boiselle, former executive assistant, Donald Doyle, Bill Neville and Michael Meighen, former national party president.

fidence in the government's budgetary policies at approximately 10 p.m. As always it was wearisome too for his appointments secretary. Wendy Orr has a busy stretch in the two or three hours following Question Period.

To hear her describe the duties of an appointments secretary sounds routine. "It's keeping the day in order more than keeping us on the button at 9.15 doing such and such," she says, "it's just seeing that things flow." But in reality all of Clark's personal appointments are funnelled through her after they are checked out with Bill Neville. Often she juggles the daily schedule after consulting with Clark because he and Neville have decided there is someone the leader should see at the last minute. Wendy Orr returned from Europe to Ottawa in December 1975, answered a newspaper advertisement which called for "a dicta-typist for a Member of Parliament," and eventually ended up working in the Clark leadership campaign. Appointed soon after Clark became leader, she has immersed herself in the job. "Occasionally I go down to Question Period," she says, "because the political system is still very new to me."

Today she is trying to finish typing up the opposition leader's schedule for the following day, a task which she performs in the late afternoon amidst scores of phone calls. The "Leader's Agenda," as it is called, has his day blocked out in time segments beginning with his departure from Stornoway and ending with his return home at night. Clark keeps his copy close by and tries to follow it to the letter.

By now, the day is nearly ended. The schedule calls for a Parliament Hill departure at 10.15 p.m. after the Commons vote, but the opposition leader has an eleventh-hour meeting with a few caucus members and his chief of staff. Tomorrow, the Horner question will be resolved one way or another. Clark and Neville bid farewell at the main entrance to the Centre Block where Oscar Henri, Clark's chauffeur, is waiting. From there, it's a fifteen-minute ride down Wellington Street toward Rockliffe and home to Stornoway, the official residence of the leader of the opposition.

Unlike many other professions, each day at the office for the leader of the opposition has its own momentum, seldom predictable but always exhilarating. Frequently he is called upon to react quickly to unforeseen developments. Similarly, each day has its own rewards, but also frustrations — which are always more difficult to bear when your own followers are the protagonists and not your defenders. Joe Clark had walked the streets in the riding of Hochelaga to help elect Jacques Lavoie in a 1975 by-election against Pierre Juneau. In the case of Jack Horner, Clark had declared after the 1976 leadership convention that he was "very conscious of the fact he [Horner] had placed fourth in the original ballot." Clark had placed third. Yet despite his attempts to make both men feel at home in the caucus, both Lavoie and Horner joined Liberal ranks, the Crowfoot member eventually becoming minister of industry, trade and commerce in the federal cabinet. The months of April and May 1977 turned out to be a bitter springtime for Joe Clark.

Party Organization

With characteristic clarity, Arthur Meighen once underlined the paramount position held by party leaders in parliamentary democracy: "I can say without reservation that the focal point of any political party in Canada is the leader. The organization is his creation and the organizer his appointee." Meighen's observation certainly applies to the present leader of the Conservative party, whose political career was built largely on organization and who spent his first year in office trying to strengthen the party throughout the country. Besides consolidating the party's fighting force in the Commons and renewing its policy development processes, Joe Clark was determined "to bring new life to Progressive Conservative organizations across Canada." Indeed, organization was one of the three short-term priorities he established just ten weeks after the leadership convention.

"There is much to be done in this regard — particularly in the province of Ontario which will be the major fighting ground in the next election," Clark told a party fund-raising dinner in Vancouver in May 1976. As national leader, he also intended "to take a strong and direct interest in that building effort in Quebec."

Clark turned to an outstanding organizer in his leadership drive to chair the leader's committee on organization. Harvie Andre, an old school mate, roomed with Clark in Ottawa after both were elected in the 1972 federal election. A chemical engineer, Andre obtained his MA at the California Institute of Technology before arriving back in Alberta in 1963. While working on his doctorate and teaching in Calgary, he became interested in the Conservative party. "When Lougheed assumed the leadership of the Alberta party we had zero seats in the legislature," Andre recalls, "and any warm bodies who were willing to work were welcomed and I got involved."

In 1971 Clark and Andre decided to become federal candidates in the election held the following year. Andre had had no intention of ever seeking office when he entered politics, preferring the backrooms and organization to his own candidacy. However, Clark encouraged him to change his mind. Douglas Harkness, a former defence minister in the Diefenbaker government, had retired from political life and his Calgary Centre seat was open to newcomers. In the 1972 campaign, Andre captured Calgary Centre by 5,500 votes over his closest rival, almost equalling Clark's margin in Rocky Mountain. Both were re-elected in 1974 and when Clark decided to run for the party's leadership, Andre was one of only two caucus members who backed his campaign. The other was Allan McKinnon, the Conservative member for Victoria.

After the leadership victory, Clark, Andre, Neville and other party strategists thoroughly analysed the country, plotting party strengths and weaknesses. Historical voting patterns now had to be applied to a new leader. Organizers also had to weigh the effects of the redistribution of federal ridings. Eventually, Clark opted for and expanded an organizational concept developed partly under Robert Stanfield. In essence, he reinforced the existing party structure with his own organizing agents in various regions of the country. Clark increased the regional organizers beyond the number Stanfield had. As a result, there are now about forty organizers across the country and they are responsible for anywhere from five to twenty-six ridings. Not all of these regional organizers supported Clark in his drive for the leadership. However, he has chosen them for their thorough understanding of the regions in which they work, and also because they can bolster normal party activity in the federal ridings.

Andre and the other caucus members representing various regions on the organization committee work closely with the regional spokesmen in organizing projects such as speaking tours for party MPs. "We don't want a fellow flying from Ottawa to Regina just to give one speech," Andre says, "we want to make use of his time there." Clark has urged caucus members to leave Ottawa and get out on the hustings more often to spread the party's message.

The leader's committee on organization flows from Clark's belief that the party must not move too quickly into a campaign mentality. In essence,

Strengthening the party apparatus: Clark, Bill Neville and Harvie Andre, the chairman of the leader's committee on organization. Andre and Clark, both elected to the Commons for the first time in 1972, represent a new breed of western politicians which have, in Clark's view, "more to offer than grievance."

it's an expansive operation. That is, the party is involved in a building strategy by trying to involve more people through memberships before it begins to recruit candidates for the next election. "There are two different functions involved in a pre-writ period," according to Bill Neville; "there is a need for a continuing program of party activity such as fund-raising and membership drives that are best done through the various party association. Then there's a more selective set of organizational priorities." These include the choosing of candidates and, in general, preparing strategy for the next election campaign.

Undoubtedly, the heavy organizational work is being done by Clark's organizers, although the two levels of activity are intended to overlap. "I think he feels that if you get into an election mentality too quickly," says Neville, "you tend to become static. So that's the reason for Andre's organization committee. With the kind of membership, mainly MPs, it's got almost a self-destruct quality in it. That is, at least once the election is called, they're not going to be here running an organization committee, they're going to be getting themselves re-elected, at which point, we will evolve to a campaign committee."

Clearly, Clark believes that a political party must be something more

On the way to caucus. With Clark are Sinclair Stevens, the party's financial critic, and Steve Paproski. In the background, from left to right, are Elmer MacKay, caucus chairman, former party leader Robert Stanfield and Ray Hnatyshyn.

than just an election-time mechanism and the party structure should be strong enough to withstand any quality of leadership. Hence, the leader's organization committee has the broad objective of strengthening the party apparatus in general, before attention is concentrated on a federal election campaign. Among its goals is the establishment of a network of Macdonald-Cartier clubs across the country. Operating in metropolitan areas for the most part, the clubs serve as recruiting vehicles for the party. They provide an opportunity for Conservatives who already belong to riding associations, and newcomers giving consideration to joining the party, to meet and communicate. The aim is to increase membership and eventually turn the federal Conservatives into the majority party in Canada. Through the Macdonald-Cartier clubs, Andre's committee is pressing constitutencies across the country towards openness. "There has been something wrong in the past," Andre says, "that the majority of Canadians have not felt comfortable with our party. We have created the impression that the Progressive Conservative party was fairly exclusive." Hence, Clark is attempting to alter this perception and welcome new members.

Andre sees a bitter irony in the fact that the Conservatives have been perceived frequently over the years as the party of big business. "Bay Street has voted both with their ballots and with their cheque books for the Liberals for thirty years but we have been carrying the political liability and it's very irritating."

With a strengthened party organization and more emphasis on preparing the constituencies for the forthcoming election campaign, the party will not be relying solely on the leader's performance. Clark realizes that campaigns have become leader-oriented and that his own campaign is vitally important. However, he believes the leader's role is to head a highly efficient force of workers with everyone contributing to their fullest capacity. It follows from this notion that the party will not live and die on the basis of Clark's personal campaign in the next election. Rather, the party hopes that, with strong local campaigns, particularly in such provinces as Ontario, British Columbia, Manitoba and Saskatchewan where it hopes to make gains, the local candidates will help to carry the leader to power as much as Clark will assist them.

Although historically the province of Quebec has been a virtual wasteland for the Tories, Clark still holds to his belief that the province must be organized like the rest of the country. When a political party consistently

does poorly in an area, it tends sometimes to seek quick solutions. The party turned to Marcel Faribault in the mid-1960s and Claude Wagner in 1972 hoping that a sizable number of seats could be won in Quebec. Clark scoffs at the idea of magical solutions and is striving to build an effective political organization in the province from the ground up. During his first year as leader, he spent considerable time in Quebec laying the ground-work for the party's organization. These visits were to show Quebeckers that he would be the party leader in their province as everywhere else. Moreover, to further symbolize his commitment to the province, Clark himself initially served as chairman of the Quebec organization committee.

After the leadership convention, the party in Quebec was badly split by the animosity that had arisen between the Wagner and Mulroney campaign

Meeting with Rene Lévesque early in 1978. This visit was a follow-up to Clark's meeting with four Conservative provincial premiers in the fall of 1977 at Kingston. Always careful to avoid harsh criticism of the Quebec government, Clark insists there will be no deals with the Parti Québecois.

workers. Both candidates had little to show for their organizational efforts in the province. "In Quebec, Clark is going to show people that there is a lot of slugging to be done," says Jodi White, "such as knocking on doors, meeting people in the street." Again, Clark appears as a leader who builds his organization slowly and carefully. His steady visits to the province have been designed to stimulate activity and, by his own presence, demonstrate his ambition to establish the party. The full extent of the impact of the 15 November Parti Québecois victory has yet to be tested federally. After the Quebec election, Clark assessed the party's standing in Quebec realistically, noting that the Conservatives have not yet established a permanent federal presence there. But he sees the party with much better prospects, because the winds of change are blowing in Quebec and a new breed of politicians is now in provincial politics.

Similarly on the federal side, Clark argues that the Conservatives have the capacity to bring into power a new range of federalist candidates in Quebec, an opportunity perhaps that the Liberals do not have. He claims that any new federalist the Liberals bring into their ranks must take second place to Jean Chretien or Marc Lalonde but, in his party, this kind of back-seat arrangement does not apply. Yet when it comes to the crunch, Clark fully realizes that his party is up against a strong Liberal organization in the province. The Conservatives have been outnumbered and out-hustled in the past, and to win even a dozen seats Clark and his party have their work cut out.

The 100,000 miles that Joe Clark travelled during his first year as leader brought him into frequent contact with party supporters, and the visits projected him as a fresh leader in the wake of the party's well-publicized leadership campaign. His trips throughout the country were aimed as much at streamlining the party's organization as they were with providing him an opportunity to meet the electorate. Like most politicians of his generation, Clark is aware that elections are actually won between campaigns in the countryside and not in the House of Commons. For this reason, he and his colleagues spend considerable time outside Ottawa establishing contact with voters. Away from the daily grind of Parliament Hill, regional visits generally provide a closer insight into a politician's personal style and relationship with the people he must have on his side.

In January 1977 Clark made his first trip as party leader to Kingston, Ontario, an area where Conservative roots go deep. He warned local

Clark addressing students at Eric Hamber high school in Vancouver in January 1977. Given Clark's youthful image, the Conservatives are aiming to increase their vote among young Canadians.

Clark meeting with students at the Queen's University Memorial Union pub in January 1977. His organizers try to create this kind of scenario, realizing that the Conservative leader is at his best on a one-to-one basis.

organizers not to be too impressed by the favourable public opinion polls, which at that time showed the Conservatives with 45 per cent of the decided voters and the Liberals with 35 per cent. He urged the party workers to capitalize on the youthful image the party was projecting. "We now have an attractiveness to younger voters," he said, "and to lower income people." In addition, Clark refused to rush into policy too quickly. "Our approach to policy cannot be taken overnight. Exquisite care is needed in the formulation of policy" — this comment perhaps prompted by the wry remembrance of the party's prices and incomes program, which had been rejected by the electorate in the 1974 campaign.

Equally revealing about the condition of the party was a comment Clark offered on his relationship to the caucus. "I would not want to have a party that did not have disagreements but I would prefer a party less public about its disagreements." This observation was a follow-up to an earlier declaration before a caucus meeting in Ottawa: "The election is ready to be won in the country. It's waiting to be lost in the caucus." Clark had proved himself, over the years, as a campaign organizer. However, now as leader, he had to solidify his hold on the caucus and, to do this, the parliamentary wing of the party had to be organized effectively. His success would depend largely on the extent to which caucus members would respond to Clark's initiatives as their new leader and party organizer.

The Caucus Cockpit

To be truly effective, a leader of the opposition must establish firm control over his caucus before engaging in combat with the government. The Conservative caucus consists of all the members of Parliament; the national director of the party; Clark's legislative assistant, Patrick Howe; and a few senators also usually attend caucus meeting. When the House of Commons is in session the caucus generally meets once a week, to discuss and decide on policies and strategy. Sometimes the debates can be highly emotional, as they provide an opportunity for each member to express his or her point of view frankly. At other times, members may show a quietly forceful manner. But since the members meet in strict privacy, one thing can always be guaranteed — caucus meetings will be intensely partisan. As the official opposition, they see themselves on the threshold of power and are single-minded in the pursuit of their objective: to defeat the government at the earliest opportunity.

Although he was far from an outstanding parliamentarian, John Bracken, the Conservative leader from 1942 to 1948, made some significant changes in the party's organization and caucus. His innovations had lasting impact. It was Bracken who first called the caucus together for a regular meeting every week, and tried to involve the full caucus in the discussion and formulation of policy. He established thirteen committees of caucus, covering such portfolios as external affairs, trade and commerce, agriculture and labour. These committees, which were divided roughly according to cabinet posts, eventually became known as the "shadow cabinet." They provided an opportunity for caucus committee members to discuss a subject before it was debated in full caucus, and allowed them to become specialists in particular areas of government activity. Presumably, the chairman of each caucus committee was a potential minister and would be ready to enter the cabinet when the Conservatives came to power.

Bracken's changes set the caucus format for subsequent party leaders by introducing a more democratic procedure and enabling the caucus to analyse legislation more thoroughly. However, the title "shadow cabinet" is a misnomer. For several reasons, the chairmen of the various committees do not in fact constitute an alternative "cabinet." As Robert Stanfield noted in a memo to caucus members in 1975: "A committee chairman has not implied a commitment to a cabinet post in the event of the party forming a government and the committee chairmen have not constituted an inner circle or decision-making group." During his years as leader, Stanfield argued strenuously against a powerful inner group of perhaps a couple of dozen caucus members paralleling the cabinet on the government side. He felt that "an opposition caucus cannot work effectively if a small group makes the decisions and struts its stuff while the great majority has no role to play except to applaud."

Of course, it must be remembered that Stanfield's position arose largely from the circumstances in the party when he assumed the leadership. There is no question that he felt that he must use most of his persuasive powers to win over the Diefenbaker loyalists who were disenchanted following the 1976 leadership race. He had also to encourage the anti-Diefenbaker members of his caucus, to revive in them a sense of purpose and usefulness that many of them had lost under the Diefenbaker regime. His solutions to these twin objectives were to divide the caucus into policy committees and delegate responsibility for party strategy as widely as possible.

When Clark became leader, he increased the number of caucus committees to thirty-two — more than twice the number under Bracken. He appointed Jim Gillies, another unsuccessful leadership contender, "chairman of chairmen" of these committees, to ensure that they would meet in a more formal way, with a specific agenda and the declared task of completing the background work on policy matters before they are introduced into caucus.

Gillies regards this new system a marked improvement on the more relaxed methods of the old days. "I always objected when I was here in 1972. I didn't see how you could work things out in a caucus of a hundred people. There was a wide variation in the way problems were handled and we didn't

A familiar scene in the leader's office on Wednesday mornings just prior to the caucus meeting. From left to right: Elmer MacKay, Steve Paproski, Clark, Ray Hnatyshyn and Walter Baker.

Jim Gillies, the chairman of chair-men and member of a special caucus group named by Clark in February 1978 to study the problems of unemployment.

have the formal structure for dealing with difficulties that overlapped; . . . the caucus committee chairmen would meet basically over lunch and it was hilarious because people would come in from all sides and there would be no agenda or anything else."

The internal structure of the caucus had a direct bearing on that fatal decision which saw the party accept a program of wage and price controls prior to the 1974 election campaign. According to Gillies, the party might have avoided that debacle if the prices and incomes program had received more careful scrutiny before the full caucus dealt with it. The Conservative caucus adopted the controversial policy in February and, in the election campaign that followed in July, found itself on the defensive. In the end, the voters rejected the Conservative proposal only to have the re-elected

Liberals introduce a version of it the following year. For Clark, and every other Tory MP, that painful electioneering experience remains indelibly stamped on their minds. They vowed after their bitter disappointment in 1974 that a more suitable vehicle had to be found whereby policy proposals could be tried out in discussion before they reached the caucus stage.

Through Gillies, who can be a demanding task master, Clark now pushes his caucus committee chairmen harder than did Stanfield, requiring a higher level of performance in the Commons and urging them to travel more throughout the country. "The chairmen are supposed to be our voice into the community on several levels," said Gillies; "one, with the people who are experts in their areas but, on top of that, they have to go out and communicate to the electorate as a whole, because they are our eyes and ears and voice out there."

Undoubtedly the committee chairmen are feeling the pinch. "Mr. Stanfield wasn't on our backs all the time the way Mr. Clark is," says Bill Jarvis, the party's critic of the solicitor general's department. "It was not highly disciplined, not because Stanfield was incapable of that but the difference with Mr. Clark is that we are much more regimented. Mr. Clark puts on the pressure and turns the screw."

The shadow cabinet Clark named in April 1976 included all the members of Parliament he had defeated at the leadership convention. Among the leading appointments were Jack Horner in transport, Sinclair Stevens in finance, Flora MacDonald in federal-provincial relations, and Claude Wagner in external affairs. John Fraser and Patrick Nowlan were named to head the labour and communications committees respectively. Clark saw the group as "a team ready and able to provide a competent, positive alternative to the present administration." Whereas Stanfield had tried to involve as many members as possible in his organization, Clark shortened the list of critics in the House to the thirty-two committee chairmen.

Clark looks to his committee chairmen for greater initiative and their policy positions, which are formulated with Jim Gillies on Tuesday afternoons, serve as a starting point for discussion the following Wednesday morning at the full caucus meeting. Clark has probably moved the Conservative party closer to a true shadow cabinet system than any party leader before him. "I've never seen the committee chairmen work so hard," says Bill Jarvis, "but you always feel that if you screw up he'll yank it from you and give it to somebody else."

Meeting of the strategy committee. Top left: John Fraser, defeated by Clark in the leadership race, is now a member of the committee and labour critic. Top right: John Laschinger, former national party director and George Hees, minister of trade and commerce in the Diefenbaker government. Bottom: Former party president Michael Meighen in earnest conversation with Bill Jarvis, the party's critic of the solicitor general's department. Seated beside Jarvis is Jean-Carol Pelletier, director of research.

Members of the strategy committee in session. Top: Walter Baker; Roch LaSalle, a principal organizer in Quebec and one of three MPs from that province; and Quebec MP Claude Wagner, runner-up to Clark for the leadership in 1976. Centre: James McGrath, caucus coordinator for social policy and named by Clark in February 1978 to head caucus group studying unemployment; and Bill Jarvis. Bottom right: George Hees, the old warrior looking for another kill.

Moreover, Clark has created a special nineteen-member strategy committee, an elite group of caucus members and party organizers who meet regularly. Stanfield had no such body within caucus because it ran contrary to the fresh tone he tried to set as leader in 1967. Besides Finlay MacDonald, Stanfield relied largely on his House leader Gerald "Ged" Baldwin, party whip Tom Bell and the then national director of the party, Malcolm Wickson, for advice on policy matters. However, they never really constituted a true strategy committee and their meetings were not regularly scheduled. The strategy committee formed by Clark is central to his new party organization. Essentially, the committee is a sounding board for the leader on both short- and long-term matters, ranging from monthly public opinion polls to the party's tactics in the next election campaign. Furthermore, the formation of the committee initially helped Clark to win over most of the defeated leadership candidates and prevent wounds from festering too long. Clark tried to strike some kind of regional balance on the committee by having members from all parts of the country. There was also a blending of experience and youth. "Normally a leader relies on his House leader and party whip," Bill Jarvis says. "They become members by virtue of their position, but Mr. Clark went beyond that. I was asked because George Hees was a senior member and I was a junior member."

While the Conservative caucus is highly active and working for the party outside of Ottawa, as Clark intended, members at times find themselves almost swamped by committee meetings. Yet they understand that greater efficiency and better performance demand this kind of frequent contact. Above all, Clark wants the profile of the caucus to be much higher than it is at present, so that the party can demonstrate its capacity to govern. He wants to avoid the situation in which the Diefenbaker government found itself in 1957. The party had only seven months between the leadership convention in 1956, where Diefenbaker was chosen to head the party, and the election campaign the following year. As a result, it had virtually no time to prepare to govern. Clark sees his caucus with a clear advantage over their colleagues of 1957. Time is on their side as they lay "the plans that would be the basis of an integrated approach to government."

To get still greater efficiency into the party's parliamentary operations, early in October 1977 Clark established six major policy areas each under the chairmanship of a senior MP. Don Mazankowski became the chief coordinator for transportation and communications; Sinclair Stevens for economic policy; James McGrath for social policy; David MacDonald for cultural policy; Allan Lawrence for food and resources; and Lincoln Alexander for government operations. This new caucus structure was aimed at producing a more coordinated attack on government policies. In another significant change, Roch LaSalle, one of three Quebec MPs, was given responsibility for unemployment, a high-profile position.

To attend a caucus meeting is an enlightening experience and provides an insight into how burdensome the role of party leader is in parliamentary democracy. Nothing could illustrate better the manifold difficulties a party leader encounters in opposition than the caucus meeting on 16 February 1977. The meeting underlined the vexation the leader faces in trying to formulate positions which will show his party as a true alternative to the existing government. Prior to ten o'clock every Wednesday morning that the House of Commons is in session, Conservative MPs leave their Commons offices for Room 371 in the West Block. On a sunny day, some will walk from the Centre Block enjoying the warm weather while others travel through the West Block tunnel. When they get to the third floor, they file down a narrow corridor to Room 371 which is closed to newsmen. In the confines of this lengthy chamber, Conservative MPs engage in what is generally free-wheeling and heated debate on a wide range of party matters. Viewpoints on particular items may differ but members have a general objective — to defeat the government and gain power. In the final analysis, everything else is subordinate to this end.

Four long rows of chairs in the caucus room form a sort of semicircle in front of a long desk where the leader sits. At the desk to his left is Elmer MacKay, the caucus chairman, who is the presiding officer of the caucus but who has no additional authority by virtue of his position. To Clark's right at the meeting is Steve Paproski, the Conservative whip, who is responsible for summoning members to caucus, seeing that all party members are present for votes and, in general, managing the party in the House. Members arrive in the caucus room only a few minutes before starting time. Some mingle to discuss the latest news reports and Parliament Hill gossip before taking their places. Others go right to their chairs and finish reading the morning newspapers before the leader arrives. On this day, Clark entered the room a minute before ten o'clock and, as is the custom, members rise to greet him.

The agenda for caucus meetings is worked out in advance by the caucus chairman in concert with the leader. At this particular meeting, the caucus

The Conservative caucus. Seated at desk at the front are, from left to right: Steve Paproski, Clark and Elmer MacKay. Walter Baker, the House leader, standing, is addressing caucus.

was scheduled to discuss the party's position on the new Fiscal Arrangements Act, Bill C-37, which contains a set of legislative proposals to alter the cost-sharing arrangements with the provinces for health and education programs. Second-reading debate was to start on Friday, only two days away. The legislation under debate would put into law an agreement Prime Minister Trudeau had reached with the provincial premiers at a first ministers' conference in December 1976. While the Fiscal Arrangements Act was a leading item, a good portion of the two-hour meeting was taken up with a lengthy debate over the issue of decentralization, which clearly showed the difficulties a party leader has in attempting to reconcile regional differences in caucus.

Clark encountered heavy criticism, principally from Ontario members,

over his call for a more decentralized form of federalism. The Conservative leader's scheme of decentralization would see the provinces gain greater control in the fields of culture and industrial development because, as he once put it, "the provincial governments are in a far better position to understand the real needs and to define objectives according to local priorities." Clark feels the federal government must be prepared to make concessions to the provinces in sectors as important as immigration and communications. An opposition leader may strive to create an alternative position to the government in power. However, as was revealed in caucus, his followers are frequently reluctant to accept his course of action when political realities peculiar to their regions have to be taken into account.

As the caucus meeting begins, Clark rises to announce the results of the latest Gallup poll, which shows the Conservatives still well ahead of the Liberals with over 40 per cent of decided voters. It is encouraging news and naturally Clark turns it to his advantage, hoping to solidify his hold on the party and keep the caucus working together as a unit. An Ontario member

Caucus meeting on 16 February 1977. Above left: Allan McKinnon, MP for Victoria, addresses caucus. Behind him, Paproski and Clark listen intently. Above: Jake Epp taking part in the debate. To his right, reading newspaper, is Paul Yewchuk.

Above: John Crosbie, the member for St. John's West, enters caucus discussion on decentralization. Seated at back on far left is the author, who watches Clark's reaction to Crosbie's arguments. Above right: Dean Whiteway, the member for Selkirk, drives home his point. Seated in front is Donald Munro.

who, unlike many in the room, knows the feeling of power from the government benches, rises to ask if the poll showed what percentage of voters remained undecided. Clark answers him while explaining to members that he thought by now the party's standing in the polls would have declined more than it has, now that the leader's honeymoon with the press is over.

The first half hour of caucus is loosely structured, providing members with an opportunity to air any grievances they may have and to suggest ways of improving the party's position in the eyes of the voters.

The meeting moves on to the Quebec by-elections which have yet to be called by the prime minister. Up to this point, Clark had been campaigning heavily in the province and was concentrating his attack on the province's economy. Whenever he spoke of national unity and the election of the Parti Québecois government, Clark had frequently tied the issue to such problems as unemployment, because he felt the Trudeau government was most vulnerable in this area. But at the caucus meeting, a Quebecker urged the Conservative leader to go further than simply discussing unemployment

Speaking in caucus on 16 February 1977. Above left: Lincoln Alexander, the member for Hamilton West. Above: Walter Dinsdale, former minister of northern affairs in the Diefenbaker government.

problems in the province. He told Clark that militants in the Union Nationale and Parti Québecois wanted a true alternative to the Trudeau government and were looking for the Tory leader to be more specific on a new distribution of powers Quebec could expect under a Conservative government. Clark listens intently to the call for him to be more precise in his statements as they relate to Quebec and the Conservative party's dealings with the separatist Parti Québecois.

When the speaker has finished, Clark rises from his chair at the middle of the large desk at the front of the room, his facial expression tightening as he surveys the caucus. Cutting the air with his left forearm, as he frequently does when speaking, his voice grows more resonant. "I will not accept, nor countenance, and I will publicly rebuke anyone who suggests we should have secret deals with the Parti Québecois." He goes on to explain that "all the party surveys and my own instincts say the by-elections will deal with economic questions."

There follows a spirited discussion over the question of decentralization, a theme that was stressed repeatedly by Clark in his drive for the party's leadership. He wants Ottawa to show greater recognition of the country's diversity. Announcing his leadership candidacy in November 1975, Clark had spelled out his position on the subject in general terms: "We should recognize that a respect for diversity is itself a form of Canadian identity. In practical terms, that means a turning away from inappropriate centralization; we must vest the provinces with the fiscal and political power to nurture vital regional and provincial and local interests, thus encouraging a regionalism that is cheerfully committed to one nation." According to Clark, "the past is gone, but among its lessons is the value of local people working together to accomplish local goals. Wherever possible, we must face our problems in that spirit, and not by creating new national bureaucracies."

These ideas may sound refreshing and convincing but selling them to caucus can be another matter. To start with, English Canadians have grown up with the belief that a strong central government is necessary in a country the size of Canada. It is often argued that only such a government can make the equalization payments necessary for the have-not provinces in Canada. Nevertheless, differences of opinion can be found over decentralization, even within a have-not province, as this caucus meeting revealed. For example, one of the Newfoundland members argued against centralism, claiming there was a clear need for more decentralization in the country. Yet a colleague from the same province saw the issue differently. This member told the caucus there was a need for a strong central government. "We have the most decentralized federation in the world," he said. Citing the Department of Regional Economic Expansion as an example, he observed that DREE cannot be decentralized any more.

Then two Ontario members, one from the southwestern part of the province and the other from the eastern region, joined the debate. The southwestern Ontario MP stood in the middle of the room, with hands on hips and his back to Clark facing the caucus. He maintained that in calling for more decentralization, the provinces were really interested in what he described as "provincialism." The eastern Ontario member was also against any further decentralization and thought an election on that issue would be unwise. When the debate subsided, Clark rose to comment on the members' remarks and to explain how the decentralization theme operates on two levels. Clark admits that the word "decentralization" can scare people. "But

I don't think the theme does," he says. Clark prefers to divide the issue into two parts. "The proposal to change the gradual gathering into Ottawa of governmental powers, where those powers are better exercised elsewhere, does not cause too much of a problem," he says. In such cultural areas as cablevision, Clark argued that "Ottawa has appropriated all powers and it has constantly undermined the undeniable rights of the provinces," a trend he would reverse.

Clark then dealt with the other side of the issue. "The other side that is tougher," he says, "is the question of industrial location. This starts being more popular out in the periphery, out on the edge where I come from, rather than the central parts of the country." The Conservative leader maintains that "it is, in fact, quite justified for the West and Atlantic and northern Canada to note that national policy, from the construction of seaways through to most transportation and tariff policy, has encouraged growth to concentrate in Canada rather than to disperse in Canada." Clark wants the national structure changed so that "provincial decisions should have priority with respect to industrial strategy."

He also thinks there have been two changes in attitude which tend to reinforce the approach he is taking on decentralization. "There is a sense that things as they are are not working and there have to be some changes. And there are changes in the ethic in the populated cores of the country." Clark found it interesting that Ontario New Democratic Party leader Stephen Lewis was able to capitalize on the concern over the industrial use of agricultural land in the 1975 provincial election campaign. Lewis promised to halt all losses of prime agricultural land through development. "There is a sense, in other words, of limits to growth," says Clark, "in the areas that have profited from growth and a sense of justice regarding the distribution of growth."

The problem of decentralization for the Tories, then, as Clark puts it, is "with the language of the proposal" and not with the theme itself. At the caucus meeting, he urged members to use the term "balanced federalism" as a substitute for decentralization, because the former does not worry people as much.

After the debate over decentralization ended, Clark called Flora Mac-Donald to the front of the room to explain the new Fiscal Arrangements Act. What had to be decided at the meeting was whether Clark would enter the debate on second reading of the bill to start on Friday and, if so, when he

The media never attend caucus but are often present before and after meetings and try to follow the workings of caucus committees. Here members of the press swarm into the caucus room as the meeting prepares to break up.

would speak in the Commons. After Miss MacDonald, the party's spokesman on federal-provincial relations, finished outlining the bill's details, Clark throws the meeting open to members. The consensus is that Clark should enter the debate because of the national implications of the proposed legislation. Two Ontario members argued that Clark should enter the debate on Friday afternoon. If he waited until the following week, they feared his speech would be lost in the heavy press coverage the prime minister would receive on his trip to Washington. In their view, Clark had no choice but to lead off for the party on Friday. An Alberta member agreed, noting that "timing is all important." Clark is in favour of leading off the debate on Friday and plans to focus his remarks not on the specific details of the bill but rather on the nature of the country which the Fiscal Arrangements Act is designed to serve. As party leader, this form of attack should give him more scope and the speech will serve as a convenient vehicle to re-enter the Confederation debate.

What this particular caucus meeting illustrated was Clark's determination to build a strong Conservative organization in Quebec, on his own, free of any formal alliances with the Union Nationale or the Parti Québecois. It also underlined Clark's sensitivity toward all regions of the country, as he sought to reassure opponents to his concept of a more decentralized federation. In dealing with their caucuses, Tory leaders over the years have adopted varying approaches which seemed to depend on their personality, ability and knowledge. Arthur Meighen would let four or five of the most outstanding members do the talking but then he would announce the policy which was to be followed. R.B. Bennett was a one-man show and simply dictated policy positions to his caucus. John Diefenbaker dominated the caucus through sheer flare and Robert Stanfield was a consensus man.

Joe Clark manages the caucus through members such as Jim Gillies and, in general, views the parliamentary wing as another body of workers to help strengthen the party's organization. "Clark does not use a heavy hand," says Bill Jarvis, "but uses Gillies very effectively and Gillies is one hell of an authoritarian when he wants to be." By enlarging the role of caucus committee chairmen and consulting with them regularly, Clark is challenging them to show they are capable of taking over the government departments for which they are responsible as critics. Clearly, party organization comes first and the caucus is secondary. "Discussion of philosophy is important, and so is our performance as an opposition in Parliament," Clark said as he launched his drive for the party leadership in November 1975, "but our essential task is to build a party which can form a national majority government. That requires active organization and a disciplined and united approach."

As a rule, Clark takes copious notes at caucus meetings. He will single out two or three members and praise or criticize the remarks they made. He is more precise in his summation at the end of caucus meetings than was Stanfield, who dealt with members' queries generally and, characteristically, was extremely patient with members, letting them speak for several minutes. Clark is more critical of comment by members and not hesitant in offending his colleagues. While he has a warm, humorous style at times, he can also be curt with a member who has advanced an unreasonable argument. On several occasions he has risen to answer abruptly, "No, that is nonsense" to proposals he finds ill conceived. He expects full attendance in the Commons at appropriate times. When it was decided at the caucus meeting that Clark would lead off second reading debate on the Fiscal Arrangements Act, he urged the caucus to be present. Full attendance would help to give the Conservative leader's speech some stature and would prevent him having to address a virtually empty chamber, as is generally the case on Friday afternoons. "It isn't the greatest time for the press gallery," Clark told the caucus. He was right. From a newsman's standpoint, the timing, of what turned out to be an important speech, was almost totally unacceptable.

Television Arrives in the Commons

When Clark rose to lead off for the opposition in the debate on the second reading of the Fiscal Arrangements bill it was the afternoon of Friday, 18 February. It would have been hard to pick a more inappropriate time for a leader to deliver a major speech. Actually, Clark's staff had been upset by the decision taken at the weekly caucus for Clark to take part at the beginning of the debate. On Friday afternoons, the only reporter generally to be found in the press gallery is the Canadian Press staffer. The rest of the Ottawa press corps are either preparing for Saturday editions or on their way to the Press Club.

The caucus did not let him down. When Clark rose to deliver what later became known as his "building" speech that Friday, there was near full attendance on the Conservative side. There were three members in the press gallery. The *Toronto Star* gave the speech front-page coverage on the following day while the *Montreal Gazette* played the story on page four. Both newspapers used CP versions of the same story.

Clark used the speech to accuse the government of dictatorial action which could only threaten Confederation.

> What we are faced with here is a fait accompli, an agreement arrived at by heads of government meeting away from here without allowing Parliament so much as an expression of opinion with regard to the options. . . .
>
> I think it is important to trace the two fundamental mistakes which this government has made when dealing with the provinces during its tenure of office. The first was, in effect, to ignore the reasons for the

federal nature of the country, to ignore the fact that only a federal system can respond to our diversity as reflected in the consistent attempt to impose Ottawa programs uniformly even where they did not fit. The second was always to treat the provinces as adversaries.

Clark then proceeded to shift the emphasis in the Confederation debate to the West, placing the results of the Parti Québecois election in a broader context.

> It is tempting to dismiss Western anger as being selfish or unjustified, just as once it was tempting to dismiss the early Quebec separatists as eccentric. . . . One of the facts of life in Canada, one of the positive facts, is that we must continually demonstrate the worth of this nation to its parts, and that challenge is alive again today in most parts of the country.

The speech was cogent but it lost media impact because of its timing. Somewhat frustrated at the lack of coverage, Clark's staff contacted newspaper editors drawing attention to their leader's remarks. The *Globe and Mail* eventually carried the speech twelve days later on page seven.

There is no question that the arrival of television in the House of Commons in October 1977 helped Clark to overcome some of his earlier problems of leadership projection. Almost overnight television raised his profile and, as is possible in the electronic age, enabled him to show that media reputations are often wrong and can be reversed. Indeed, for Joe Clark, the live television coverage of parliamentary debate was timely, because he was about to enter the recovery stage of his leadership.

To understand the effect of television on Clark's leadership, a brief retrospective look at the impact of the medium on Canadian politicians is, perhaps, necessary. First of all, federal politicians over the years have approached television with caution both during and between election campaigns. Their instinct generally has been to contain it, to limit its use while clinging on the hustings to the ways of the past. In 1957 John Diefenbaker had used television extremely effectively, as did Pierre Trudeau in 1968. But these two campaigns represent the high points in the history of media politics in Canada. Seldom would Canadian politicians break ranks and experiment with television unless pressed to do so by their media advisers. Even then most federal politicians accepted innovation grudgingly. Politicians seek to conserve power and in wanting more are unwilling to change what they already have. Just as in the early days of radio, public acceptance of television ran ahead of the willingness of politicians to experiment with it. Not surprisingly, any proposal to admit TV cameras into the House of Commons was postponed over and over again.

Back in February 1968 when Joe Clark was working in the office of his predecessor, Robert Stanfield, television changed the country's political life. It was then that the Liberal government headed by Lester Pearson was defeated in the Commons on a tax bill. On this occasion Pearson, who had to hurry back from holidays to deal with the parliamentary crisis, accepted the advice of Romeo LeBlanc, his press secretary. LeBlanc, a former CBC French-language television correspondent in Washington, persuaded Pearson to put his arguments for a reprieve for his government directly to the nation on television. The strategy worked. After the prime minister had made his appeal to the people, opposition members received a heavy mail from constituents urging them to end the parliamentary crisis and let the government get on with running the country. "As far as the man in front of his TV set was concerned," wrote Arnold Edinborough, "an unpopular tax had been voted down, the Liberals accepted the fact and were prepared to go on to other things."

It was the first time that a procedural wrangle in Parliament had been settled by popular vote. Viewers simply rejected the call by the Tories and New Democrats for an election. Pearson's use of the medium, his most skilful ever, was a lesson to all political parties. Television seemingly had become more potent than Parliament and the latter never recovered from the onslaught of the electronic media. Yet the cameras would not make their way into the Commons for almost another decade.

The Conservative government headed by John Diefenbaker in 1957 had brought about the first televising of the opening of Parliament in the fall session of that same year. But the cameras did not stay long. By this time, television in Canada was only five years old and, although the public saw it as a new source of entertainment and knowledge, politicians tended to perceive it differently. The majority of them seemed more intent on harnessing the medium for their own advantage rather than introducing it into the Commons where television would allow the electorate to see their elected members at work.

And so the "scrum" was born in the foyer of the Commons, then later

The scrum in Room 130-S. For Clark it has not proved a satisfactory vehicle for communication with a mass electorate.

moved to Room 130-S in the Centre Block on Parliament Hill. It was television at its worst — the talking head — and, as Diefenbaker frequently reminded Canadians, a terribly inexact method of reporting what had taken place in the Commons, the national forum where the leading issues of the day supposedly receive careful scrutiny. Canadians who watched the 11 p.m. network newscasts saw the politician buried in a forest of microphones. Even members of the print medium began relying on tape recorders, realizing that the fallible human memory cannot compare to the precision of electronics. Throughout the 1960s and until the advent of TV in the Commons, the scrum remained a phony mock-up where distortions and inaccuracies frequently occurred, as politicians revised and edited their earlier statements in the Commons.

Undoubtedly the scrum presented Clark with a major problem. He was often disappointed with his performances when he later watched the network newscasts. Despite attempts by his staff to help him tighten his remarks for the thirty-second clip required for television, Clark appeared stiff and rigid. The format simply did not allow his strengths to show. As Murray Coolican, his former director of scheduling, explained, "People watching TV got the feeling that Clark was lecturing to them. They didn't get the feeling of a guy who was prepared to listen." However, the scrum was not the true source of the problem. Bill Neville related Clark's earlier problems of projection to the office of the leader of the opposition. "The problem with the national news," he says, "is you're almost always on there as the critic and so it's a negative kind of thing. You're always on there because you've got a sense of outrage about something so that you're hyped up by definition." So the scrum, in Neville's opinion, "was intrinsically not a good communications vehicle for the leader of the opposition."

As it still is now with cameras in the Commons, the objective of appearing in the scrum was to get the leader a slice of footage on the television newscasts at night time with their large audiences. This strategy is dictated by the simple fact that out there is where the voters are. In its 1970 report, the Senate Committee on the Mass Media noted that "two in three Canadians watch the news daily on television and more than nine in ten watch television news at least once a week." Moreover, television is the most believed medium for Canadian news of national importance. Getting on the network news is now for politicians a matter of the highest priority.

In 1970 the Commons Procedure and Organization Committee began struggling with the problem of bringing television into the Commons. The Committee's recommendations were tabled in June 1972 and it was hardly surprising that there was an extremely cautious tone to its findings. Members agreed in principle with the broadcasting of proceedings of legislative assemblies and their committees but felt that "certain further steps should be taken before a final report is made." The following year, in the Speech from the Throne in January, the Trudeau government announced its intention to introduce full broadcast coverage of Parliament. Like the Commons Procedure and Organization Committee, the Liberals wanted all-party consent before proceeding on the controversial issue. Re-elected in the 1974 federal campaign, the government spent the next two years studying the impact of television on the United Nations and provincial legislatures. Finally, in 1977, an ultra-modern television control room was installed in the House of Commons, the masterwork of a $4.8 million project to allow broadcasting of Parliament. The politicians had finally given in and television was triumphant. Joe Clark, as a relatively new leader, now had a new vehicle to break through whatever barrier still existed between him and the electorate. Moreover, he had an opportunity to regain some of the ground lost through months of unfavourable publicity.

First of all, Clark's tours around the country often seemed to lack purpose and he delivered important speeches in inappropriate places. An example of this was his address to a public meeting sponsored by the Vegreville Conservative Association in Lloydminster, Alberta on 21 May 1976, a Friday night. The federal budget was to be brought down the following Tuesday and Clark went to great lengths to outline what he felt the budget should contain. Unfortunately for a political leader seeking news coverage, a Friday night speech is next to hopeless. "It's the worst possible time to make a speech," says Bill Neville; "in terms of the media, he might as well have been in Inuvik. Yet of the three or four most significant speeches during his first year, I think at least two of them were on Friday night. Those are the kinds of mistakes we've made, technical mistakes which seem small in themselves but which add up to a problem and those are the kind of things we have corrected."

Clark's aides initially faced difficulty in trying to create the kind of scenarios which would show his qualities positively. There was considerable trial and error before they realized that Clark is far more effective in small groups than in large audiences. As Jodi White puts it, "The prime minister seems to be much better the bigger the crowd gets. Clark is effective on a one-to-one basis. He is not good in big crowds." So during Clark's "look and learn" tours around the country, the emphasis has shifted toward small groups of people away from large numbers.

Not only did Joe Clark come from obscurity to capture the leadership, but he went through also more than a year as party head without clearly defining his policy positions. Hence, there was a vacuum when Clark toured the country. In many instances, the public perception of Clark fostered by the media was negative. Part of the blame must rest with Clark himself. He expressed no desire to rush into policy announcements. Instead he talked for months about a policy advisory council which he planned to set up to help his party prepare for the job of governing Canada. Jim Hawkes, Clark's

Waiting for the staged reply of the Commons proceedings. According to Clark, "with the exception of surprise that exists in Parliament, the media are any politician's major adversary."

former policy adviser, who was replaced by Duncan Edmonds, feels Clark made an error in saying loud and clear he was going to hold back on policy statements. Hawkes argues that Clark's expressed reluctance to define himself and his party on policy matters encouraged the media to portray him as an empty figure. Clark himself now realizes his mistake. In politics, the impression the public receives is what ultimately counts. "Joe Who" eventually became "Joe What."

However, there was still another reason for some of Clark's failures during the first year and a half of his leadership. That was the indirect criticism levelled at him by the Liberal party and spread effectively throughout the country. "They criticized him indirectly," says Duncan Edmonds, "by saying something like this: well, yeah I know we haven't done all that great a job and Trudeau has some weaknesses and there is this problem and that problem. But you know, on balance, would you take a 37-year-old kid who can't hold his caucus together? On balance, there is no alternative. Yet I don't know where in this country you could find anybody else at age 37 who has the range of skills and qualities that Joe Clark has."

This criticism and media assault on the Conservative leader reached a high point during the months of April, May and June 1977. With caucus upheavals and polls sagging steadily, Clark confessed to feeling more than a shade harassed and operating at nerve ends. "I do think that there is a cyclical effect to media in this country which I think is healthy," Clark said during this period, "their bias is generally against the guy who is up and that means they soon should turn to me." It was an accurate forecast. His hard days were just about behind him.

On 5 July Clark gave one of his strongest speeches ever in the Commons during the debate on national unity. It was an extremely well-structured speech and contained what strategists call "good code words," which mean different things to different people but bring comfort to both sides. Since Clark pleased most members of his caucus with the speech, his effort started the caucus consolidation. He challenged the government's "concept that language and language policy will unify Canadians." To the contrary, Clark argued that "bilingualism or having two languages, by definition does not unite. It divides. It is a necessary goal, but it is not the glue: bilingualism is not the glue which will hold this country together." He went on to urge the government "to build Canadian unity, not on the basis of bilingualism or of language differences but despite bilingualism, which is an important, continuing part of the policy of this land."

Stepping up his earlier call for a more decentralized federalism, Clark charged that Ottawa "has appropriated all powers and it has constantly undermined the undeniable rights of provinces in cultural areas. This trend will have to be changed and the sooner the better." The Conservative leader asked "Is it going to wreck the country if Saskatchewan gains some say in cablevision, or if Quebec does?"

"What is at issue here," Clark told the Commons, "is not just the future of one province but the concept of our whole, large country. Of course we need a strong central government to establish economic policy and to meet other common needs. But we also need strong provincial governments, strong local governments and a strong private sector to meet needs and develop potentials that are not common across Canada. We are an uncommon country. We differ from place to place, from person to person."

The speech was well received in the party and in the country. It was the first of four important developments for Clark prior to the advent of television in the Commons. The second was the Kingston communique of 16 September which followed after Clark had met with the four strongest and most prominent Conservatives in the country. Meeting with Conservative premiers Lougheed, Moores, Davis and Hatfield in the historic city hall in Kingston, Ontario, the five leaders agreed to basic constitutional changes designed to promote economic growth throughout the country, but which would not create a special language status for Quebec. This stand was clearly at variance with the recent proposal announced by Prime Minister Trudeau in which minority language rights would be written into the constitution with a special provision for Quebec limiting freedom of choice in that province. After the meeting, Clark said, "We can't accept opting in and out on something so fundamental as human rights."

For Clark, the Kingston meeting was an important symbolic occasion and a mild triumph. It was the first time that he had met with the four Tory premiers to coordinate national policy. His success at Kingston sent another message back to the caucus and the party. Moreover, the Kingston meeting was the start of the media turnaround for Clark.

Then came the thunderclap on 22 September 1977. Clark's predecessor, Robert Stanfield, told John Diefenbaker to shut up and "stop sticking a knife" into the party leader. Diefenbaker had criticized Clark's leadership by publicly announcing that he voted for Quebec Conservative MP Claude Wagner in the 1976 party leadership race won by Clark. "Whether or not John Diefenbaker or Bob Stanfield voted for Mr. Clark at the leadership convention is now quite irrelevant," said Stanfield. "Mr. Clark deserves our support as leader." The Conservative caucus remained conspicuously silent. No one came to Diefenbaker's defence. Clark naturally stayed out of the exchange between Stanfield and Diefenbaker but regretted "that the media concentrate their attention exclusively on imagined problems of the party and not on our proposals or on our call for a new budget."

On 11 October Clark received yet another boost when the provincial

The Dunning Trust Lecture in Kingston, Ontario, on 20 January 1977. Clark addressed students and faculty at Grant Hall on the campus of Queen's University. After his speech, he fielded questions from the audience, one of his favourite campaign formats.

Conservatives defeated the NDP government of Ed Schreyer in Manitoba. It was a good omen for the federal Conservative leader. As Charles Lynch observed:

> The Conservative victory in Manitoba reflects a swing to the right, across the country, if we set aside Quebec as a special case. Five of the ten provincial governments are Conservative — Newfoundland, New Brunswick, Ontario, Manitoba, and Alberta. Three of the others are small-c conservative in their attitudes — Social Credit in British Columbia, and Liberal in Nova Scotia and Prince Edward Island. Even in Saskatchewan, the sole remaining province with an NDP government, it is the Conservative party that is on the rise. Provincially, the Liberals are in trouble everywhere — in some cases, as witness the Manitoba election result, the party has virtually ceased to exist.

Hence, a week or so before television entered the Commons, Clark had acquired a new confidence after the dismal summer months. His Commons speech on national unity, the Kingston communique, Stanfield's rebuke of Diefenbaker and the Manitoba election result helped him immeasurably. Nevertheless, when he rose to speak in the Commons on television and showed his effective debating skills, Canadians naturally were somewhat puzzled. They wondered where the skinny, knock-kneed kid from High River had gone. Joe Clark now had a new image, this time a favourable one.

Like any political leader, Clark scans the horizon continuously for any possible advantage. The nature of the Question Period in the Commons, particularly during the first days of the televised proceedings, gave him a decided edge. It tends to favour the interrogator, and with the economy reeling, a sagging Canadian dollar and RCMP scandals, Clark had an opportunity to show he was at least equal and sometimes superior to the prime minister. The media do not have the staffs to cover Ottawa properly and to thoroughly report on the inner workings of government departments. Important bills frequently do not get the detailed scrutiny they deserve. The media focus their attention on the daily Question Period because here is drama, excitement and the element of surprise.

Clark himself is fully aware of the major role Question Period has come to play in parliamentary democracy. "Question Period's appeal for the media," he has written, "is its brevity and drama. Their attention to it, and avoidance of other debates, fosters the public impression that Parliament is

Clark examines his upcoming schedule at night aboard a chartered aircraft while on one of his "look and learn" tours of the country.

a place for excitement and anger, but hardly for serious discussion. It is a disappointment to find that when I or those in the Progressive Conservative party with responsibilities as departmental critics rise to outline our detailed positions in debate, the media representatives are often absent and the coverage scanty."

There is a peculiar chemistry to the hour or so when the opposition probes the government. Both government and opposition view the Question Period as an opportunity to create pseudo-events in the hope that they will tickle the media's fancy in the process. The confusion of news with theatre is particularly pronounced in the reporting of parliamentary news.

Bill Neville looks upon the Question Period as "80 per cent media exercise." His observations show the irrelevancy of Parliament in a televisual age. "Let's be honest," he says, "the government doesn't look on it as an opportunity to give information. I don't know why we should look on it as an opportunity to get it. And so I think you look at an issue not only in terms of what you might do in the House but in what way is that going to catch the imagination of the Press Gallery." Even with television cameras now inside the Commons, both the government and opposition will continue to look on Question Period mainly as an opportunity to gain media exposure.

Clark wasted little time playing to the new TV audience. Recognizing the depressed economy was a Conservative ally, Clark charged that "among the Canadians who are watching us here now are a large number of the army of Canadian unemployed who, because of the policies of this government, have nothing else they can do with their time today." The next federal election campaign was on. Almost overnight Canadians gained a renewed interest in Clark. It was a letter to the editor in the *Montreal Star* which clearly explained the advantage Clark enjoyed with the advent of TV in the House.

Clark in action in the Commons. This is the revitalized image of the leader that now appears on television screens in homes across the nation.

> Prime Minister Trudeau, with his up-front...personal style, does very well when spoken to directly. His soft quips can be heard, his understatement appreciated. Opposition leader Joe Clark, by contrast, sounds boomingly wooden....But how it all changes in the storm of parliamentary cock-fighting, with the heckling, the cheers and general hubbub. In this situation, Mr. Clark has a commanding presence. Instead of sounding pompous...his speech carries above the hurly-burly of the crowd...The reasoned, even cool nature of Trudeau's delivery hardly makes it past the background noise of the House....

Clark no longer had to rely solely on the scrum to remain visible. Those previous static shots with the glum background in Room 130-S were replaced by live televison with better camera angles which gave the television picture greater depth and showed Clark's fiery debating style.

It will take several years before the full impact of televison in the Commons can be assessed. But, for the moment, the first impression of Clark had been a positive one. In 1974 Walter Stewart had written that when "the House of Commons rumbles into order, his slender arms become batons, his eyes flash, his voice deepens and the public Joe Clark emerges as an eloquent, forceful, dynamic personality. Presence; you have it or you don't; Joe Clark has it." Now Canadians could see for themselves; and those who didn't catch a glimpse of the Conservative leader during the first week of this new age of political broadcasting heard about him from their neighbours.

Packaging

When he had appeared as the guest on CHUM radio's talk show program in January 1977, Clark faced a number of calls from listeners suggesting various ways he could remake his image as the new Conservative leader. A woman caller told him to get his hair styled. "You're so cute," she said. Sounding slightly embarrassed by it all, Clark laughed and responded that he was "not going to get it styled." However, a week after television had entered the Commons, Clark was sporting a new look following a visit to a Toronto hair stylist. A shorter cut with a part in the left side tended to soften his appearance. When Clark realized that he would be seen more frequently with cameras in the House, he apparently changed his mind about hair styles.

Indeed there had been scores of suggestions put to Clark by ad men and others who were searching for an image which would truly personify the leader of the opposition. He was urged to grow a mustache or even a beard. The beard, it was felt, would solve several problems — masking both his youth and his receding chin — and it would also impart an air of mystery to him. But Clark scoffed at such proposals. He admits to little faith in advertising agencies or image-makers. His wait of almost two years to have his hair styled is indicative of how reluctant he is to accept the dictates of ad men.

"You might have to do something to stop your hair from blowing around," he said in June 1977, "but I personally think that is a mistake. I think people want somebody natural and if they look like they've been pre-packaged I think that is resented." Curious language from a leader who learned politics in the 1960s, an age of televison, style and political imagery.

As Sandra Gwyn perceptively observed, "Clark's style, which maybe is the right match for this dissident and querulous era, is to have no style."

While he considers ad men to be almost anathema because of their penchant for merchandising, Clark knows that political leaders cannot afford to ignore the new methods of communicating with the electorate. The mass media, television in particular, has played a large part in eroding the party system in Canada to the point where Canadians now respond more to leaders than to parties. Clark observed this in a private member's bill which he introduced in December 1974, in which he called for a parliamentary committee to study the "powers, prerogatives and privileges" of the Prime Minister's Office. Clark recognized that presidential politics had come to Canada.

Yet despite his dislike for advertising agencies, Clark, like other party

On the phone to regional organizers in a London hotel room in February 1978. Clark prefers to spend an hour or two alone before an evening speaking event. Later he addressed a dinner meeting of West London Jaycees.

Clark enjoying a candlelight dinner with party organizers in the Eastern Townships of Quebec.

leaders, has no choice but to adjust to the more sophisticated campaign techniques which have dominated election campaigns in Canada since the early 1960s. To try to comprehend the struggle which Clark and any major political figure of the mid-1970s faces in his dealings with the mass media, we must understand how changing campaign methods have placed new demands on politicians.

During much of the nineteenth century and for the first quarter of the twentieth, the newspaper was the central and most influential medium of mass communication in Canadian society. Initially radio was not a serious challenger. Unlike the bland organs of today, the newspapers which circulated in Canada in the half-century after Confederation were highly partisan journals. Prominent publishers included Clifford Sifton of the *Manitoba Free Press*, Joseph Atkinson of the *Toronto Star* and Hugh Graham of the

Montreal Star, men of immense political influence. Parties saw notable advantage in aligning themselves with publishers upon whom they could rely for editorial support.

The birth of broadcasting altered the politician-publisher symbiosis but the change was slow in coming. It took the politicians several elections to recognize the advantage radio could bring them. When the shift of emphasis finally began, it was assisted by an important change in the newspaper industry itself, which transformed the metropolitan dailies into great business enterprises. This change somewhat reduced the power of the press in the political arena. The big dailies not only began to look to politically neutral wire services for news but also strove to trade on "impartiality" in return for more advertising revenue and expanded readership. It was in these circumstances that radio began to alter the style of federal election campaigns.

Until the early 1950s, the rate of change in broadcasting technology was relatively slow, the most important developments being the steady increase in the number of radio stations operating in the country and the improvement in audio recorders. In this period, an important development took place which had one of the most profound impacts on political broadcasting in Canada until televison arrived. The federal election campaign in the fall of 1935, four years before Joe Clark was born, introduced political soap opera to Canadian radio in the form of "Mr. Sage." Living in a small Ontario town, the argumentative Mr. Sage was a lifelong supporter of the Tories with a sharp distaste for Grits. In six broadcasts, lasting either fifteen or twenty minutes, Mr. Sage discussed the issue of the campaign with Mrs. Sage in a manner that suggested ordinary home conversation. The first of the broadcasts originated in a studio of the Canadian Radio Broadcasting Commission at 805 Davenport Road in Toronto, which the J.J. Gibbons Advertising Agency had rented for the occasion. The broadcast was fed from the studio to a nation-wide network of Canadian stations which included CFRB and CKCL Toronto. The national network which carried the broadcast included a number of the stations of the publicly owned Canadian Radio Broadcasting Commission. Liberal organizers could later find only one of the Mr. Sage scripts but the following, from the second broadcast, reveals the flavour of the series:

"Mother, I think Mr. King might have been a great Patriot like Laurier." "Ah, there was a great man." Yes, Ma, and "what a contrast

Meeting some of Canada's future voters. Above right: In the Medway High School cafeteria in Arva, near London, Ontario. At least one member of Clark's office staff travels with him on regional visits. In this case it is Patrick Howe (with beard). On Howe's left is John McGarry, regional organizer for the party. Bottom right: Enjoying fish and chips with the Medway High School students. Clark expects southern Ontario ridings to be crucial in the next election.

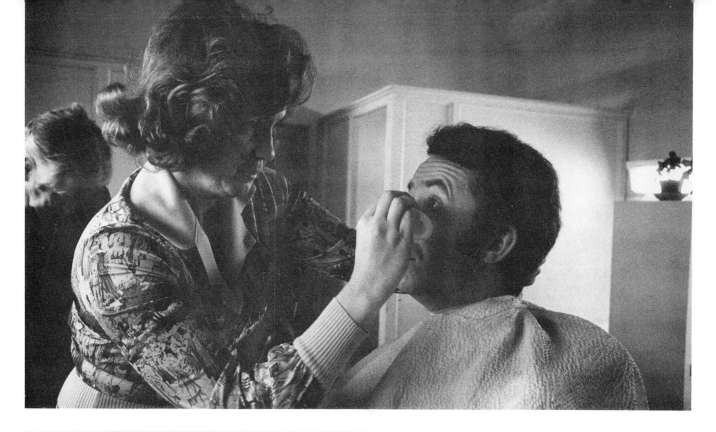

Makeup for the TV camera at CBOT studio in Ottawa. For the most part Clark shuns this kind of artificiality, though recognizing the importance of appearance in communicating with impressionable voters.

Clark and Neville listen to questions from callers on CHUM talk show in Toronto, January 1977.

to Mr. King." "Laurier was a leader everybody respected whether they agreed with him or not. He wouldn't have stooped to play petty old politics when Canada's welfare was at stake. He was a Patriot first and Mr. King might have been a patriot too if it hadn't been for his constant fear. Fear, Pa, constant fear of losing his job."

Mackenzie King was not amused. Following his triumphant return to office he had the entire Sage episode investigated to determine who was responsible for the broadcasts. A new broadcasting act in 1936 clamped tight restrictions on political broadcasting, including the prohibition of dramatization. These regulations effectively stymied innovation in the political use of the electronic media in Canada until the 1960s. Politicians and their media advisers had to follow rigid formats, as did the broadcasters themselves. Not until the introduction of television were the legislative strictures in the 1936 Broadcasting Act overcome, forcing politicians to adapt to this new form of communication.

If a single event marked the shift of emphasis from radio to television in Canada, it was the Progressive Conservative leadership convention of December 1956. CBC radio had provided extensive coverage of the 1948 convention which had chosen Louis St. Laurent leader of the Liberal party. Eight years later both radio and televison registered John Diefenbaker's triumph. In 1957 Diefenbaker ousted the Liberal government of St. Laurent and television ousted radio as the political medium of national attention. Henceforth, radio would be used by politicians mainly on a local or regional basis. Moreover, with the advent of television, advertising agencies assumed an enlarged role in Canadian political life. The 1962 election in Canada saw them front and centre on the campaign stage. Although ad agencies had participated in the planning of election campaigns in Canada as early as the 1930s, their importance in Canadian politics was not very great until this particular campaign. Significantly, it was an American event — the smooth presidential campaign of John F. Kennedy — that aroused Canadian interest.

Clark is inclined to play down the style side of politics and the impact of the Kennedy years. "You can't become something you aren't because in that regard the medium of TV can pick up any falseness," he says. "Style was a concept which I suppose Kennedy brought in, although when you look back at a Harry Truman he seemed to deliberately do things which personified him."

Nevertheless, after Kennedy's convincing demonstration of the use to which the electronic media could be put in the service of political power, American methods and techniques of campaign management made great headway in Canada. In the previous decade, advertising agencies in the United States had become highly skilled in nearly all aspects of campaign operation. Indeed, political advertising had evolved from a simple craft to a complex skill. Accordingly, rank and file aspirants to public office in the United States had come to rely more on campaign specialists than on party strategists for political advice. Advertising agencies in Canada naturally watched this evolution with considerable interest. Soon they were recruiting personnel who could offer the same campaign expertise as their U.S. counterparts in return for healthy contracts. The attitude of the agencies reflected a strong feeling in the Canada of the early 1960s that the country had graduated from the steam age of radio to the nuclear age of television.

Hence party leaders are now widely thought of as people who must understand, if they are to succeed, the fundamentals of radio and television performance. Mackenzie King, for example, approached radio with caution and never had to contend with television; perhaps to his great disadvantage Louis St. Laurent manifested a distaste for television. By contrast, Pierre Trudeau is generally looked upon as an accomplished radio and television performer although, in some observers' eyes, he fell short of expectations during the first week of live television in the Commons. However, it has been estimated that Trudeau is seen by more people in some weeks than King and St. Laurent were in their whole careers. Clark has measured his opponent accurately and knows that he must make better use of the media to overcome the restraints of the office of the leader of the opposition. But he wants to do so on his own terms and not with an advertising agent shouting directions at him.

Clark's essential problem is that he is a leader born out of power. "Part of my political difficulty which I think we can overcome," he says, "is that I am up against a man who has been in office very prominently, not quietly in office, but prominently in office for the last decade and there is a deeper definition good and bad of him." Moreover, Clark realizes that Pierre Trudeau has utilized the media extraordinarily well. He has removed himself from the scrum and his regular news conferences give him better control of the flow of information to the public. The prime minister, by the nature of his office, commands more media attention. The Conservative

Clark is an incessant coffee drinker. He is shown here sipping away during a hotline program on CKWS radio in Kingston, Ontario, in January 1977.

111

The loneliness of the campaign trail. Above: Clark eating alone in his suite at the Edmonton Plaza Hotel. Left: An exhausted Clark takes a nap en route to the next speaking engagement.

party counters by making use of the media whenever opportunity offers while getting maximum mileage out of Clark's performances in the Commons. "I think we can develop an awareness of who I am," Clark says, "but I don't think we can do that artificially, I think we have to make use of the media available to us."

Reluctantly Clark wears makeup for the television camera. He regularly makes guest appearances on talk shows to reach a wide cross-section of voters and has even had electronic equipment installed in his office to enable him to participate in open-line programs while at work.

Clark must place himself in the hands of party advancemen who are, in many ways, the embodiment of the sophisticated organization so apparent in today's election campaigns. These young agents are generally lawyers, brokers or business executives on leave from their regular jobs during election campaigns. They are responsible for getting the crowds out, making sure the bands play on time, and above all ensuring that the leader is on schedule. If Clark is hand-shaking his way through a crowd, they will speed him up or slow him down depending on the time available. Efficiency is their watchword. Their function is to get the leader maximum exposure with minimum strain on him. When an advanceman is being trained for the job, the Conservative party demands that he grasp the contents of a thick book, which is appropriately coloured in blue, entitled *Tour Manual for Advance People*. The material contained in this guide shows how much the media do not see and how little of what comes over the television screen is left to chance.

"In any successful local event," advancemen are told, "the local organizers will be the instruments for smooth functioning events. You will be the key but you must be the hidden key. All advance persons must be extremely careful to maintain a low profile." On the subject of crowds, the manual reads: "Getting huge wildly enthusiastic crowds out to every event will be one of the greatest difficult challenges to your personal wit and ingenuity. Take every possible advantage of built-in crowds. Include the leader in every appropriate local event where there will already be crowds." Other strictures: do not appear to be "too efficient. We are constantly referred to by the media as those ambitious young aides in blue suits, surrounding the leader. Rightly or wrongly, this type of image merely fuels the media's imagination glands....Also, do not play 'Hail to the Chief' when the leader enters a hall and if a walk-on is used, the introduction should consist of only these words — 'Ladies and Gentlemen, I give you the next Prime Minister of Canada, Joe Clark.'"

Not surprisingly, this kind of highly structured tour occasionally produces tensions within the party, because local organizers and workers are frequently by-passed. Regardless of any local initiatives when the leader tours an area, the final decisions for getting him from one place to another rest with the advancemen. Even before Clark leaves Ottawa every step of the way is planned and organized by the tour group in his office, leaving little margin for error. The confidential staff memos outlining the itinerary detail how Clark will be introduced at specific events by local officials and also allot the leader a certain time frame for shaking hands with people in attendance. In fact, these memos even advise him on the clothes he should wear.

The itinerary for the leader also shows that the Tories are discreet in their selection of talk-show hosts. The John Gilbert show on CHUM radio, where Clark made a guest appearance, is a popular hotline program with a large female audience. "Mr. Gilbert," the memo reads, "is a strong Tory who openly advocated the election of [Premier] Bill Davis during the last provincial election." Hotline shows made great headway in the late 1960s, presumably because they served as a vehicle for the man in the street to speak his mind. But they required of politicians yet another potentially traumatic adaptation. The destructive potential of the hotline format was shown in the 1972 campaign when former Conservative leader Robert Stanfield appeared on CFRS radio in Simcoe, Ontario, and received no phone calls from listeners — a sobering thought for all party leaders who wish to use this campaign weapon.

It was hardly surprising that Clark should choose his long-time friend Lowell Murray as his national campaign chairman for the next federal election. Since 1956 when he wrote speeches for Conservative candidates in the Nova Scotia provincial election, Murray has been highly active as an organizer. Following that election which ended twenty-three years of uninterrupted Liberal rule and saw Robert Stanfield elected premier, Murray went to Montreal where he wrote speeches for Donald Gordon, president of Canadian National Railways. Later he returned to Nova Scotia and was unsuccessful in the 1960 provincial election when he sought to defeat the leader of the CCF. Throughout the 1960s, Clark and Murray worked together in every federal election either as speech-writers or on the organizational side

Clark's tours are organized down to the last detail, so that no opportunity to meet the people will be wasted. Top: A big stretch during a hotline show in Vancouver. Clark talks to Dennis Ververgaert of the Vancouver Canucks following the game in January 1977. Bottom: Autograph seekers at a Ukrainian dinner in Montreal. Mainstreeting in Kingston, Ontario.

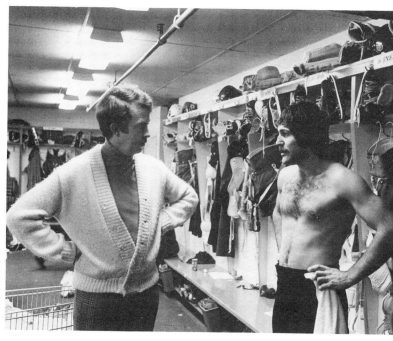

Chatting with two delegates to the Conservative convention in Quebec City in November 1977. Below: Speaking to senior citizens in the Toronto riding of Rosedale in January 1977. The riding is one to watch in the next election, when Toronto Mayor David Crombie is expected to be the Conservative candidate against Dr. John Evans, president of the University of Toronto, for the Liberals.

of the campaigns. When the pair were not engaged in trying to bring the federal Tories to power, frequently they would be off holidaying in Europe. After Clark decided to run as a candidate in 1972, Murray turned his attention to New Brunswick, becoming top adviser in the office of Premier Richard Hatfield from 1974 to 1976.

Murray firmly believes that a campaign chairman has to have a thorough knowledge of the situations in which the party leader will be comfortable. "It's how well the campaign chairman knows the leader. In this kind of role, which I have played in federal and provincial politics before, I have found that the important thing is to have an insight into his thinking, then you can usually tell how he will react in a given situation." To use the advertising terminology, the "packaging" of Joe Clark rests largely with Murray, a man the leader obviously feels has a sense of proportion about campaign strategy.

It has been said that the point of view of the newly powerful media specialists in the television age is that politics is too important to be left to politicians. As John Laschinger, a former IBM data centre manager, succinctly puts it: "The caucus, with all respect, does not understand the nuts and bolts of a campaign. They don't understand a tour, they don't understand media."

Laschinger, who resigned as the party's national director after Murray denied him a senior position on the election campaign committee, used to boast that he organized the first political leadership convention in Canada that did not lose money. The party broke even on its 1976 convention which cost $650,000 after running a deficit of $264,000 following the 1967 convention. "Lasch," as he was known in party circles, served as one of twelve advancemen who worked for William Davis in the 1971 Ontario election and later for Robert Stanfield in 1972 and 1974. The group was part of what became known as the Big Blue Machine, a coterie of non-elected officials who specialized in the various intricacies of campaigning. "It was just a bunch of guys who had a lot of fun, had track records in other areas, that had been asked to help out and do things," says Laschinger. "That was the Big Blue Machine." However, Laschinger is modest in his description. The Big Blue Machine brought a managerial revolution to Canadian politics — a revolution which seems to have at its core the notion of the politician as just one more consumer product who must be "sold" to the people.

Whatever the validity of this notion, it was hard to argue with the success which the smooth Conservative organization had in the 1971 Ontario election. The Big Blue Machine delivered the province to the Tories intact for another four years in what advertising executive Norman Atkins, one of the masterminds behind the machine, described as a storybook campaign in terms of communication and organization. The following year this same group of organizers, who had been the driving force behind William Davis' campaign in Ontario, almost managed to elect Robert Stanfield as prime minister. The final results of the 30 October 1972 election were: Liberals 109, Conservatives 107, NDP 31, Socred 15, and two independents. In Ontario alone, the Conservatives were able to pick up twenty-three seats from the Liberals.

There was a marked similarity between the two campaigns. The Davis campaign and Stanfield's Ontario campaign operation were conducted from the same headquarters in Toronto. Instead of the dozen or so advancemen used in the provincial campaign, sixty of them coordinated Stanfield's cross-Canada tour. New techniques which had been introduced in the Ontario election were applied federally. For example, in the provincial campaign, the party set up its own company known as Ad Hoc Enterprises to do all television commercials and free-time programming on the two major Canadian networks. The federal wing of the party established an operation similar to Ad Hoc in the 1972 campaign known as Promotional Advertising Creative Enterprises or PACE for short.

After the 1972 campaign, the federal Tories found themselves drained both in people and financial resources. "If you want to look at a fundamental cause for our difficulty in 1974," says Harvie Andre, chairman of the leader's committee on organization, "it was that." The Big Blue Machine, fresh after its outstanding success in 1971 had stepped in federally and had performed well for Robert Stanfield. But with another federal campaign coming just two years later, the party found itself thin on campaign workers and money. "We've got to be deeper," argues Andre, "we've got to have more to draw on and that is what we're aiming at."

Despite its high level of organization, the machine was a source of irritation among some party workers who felt excluded from campaign strategy. With the major campaign decisions largely made in Toronto by a group of advertising specialists, the campaign appeared to be taken out of the hands of the party. Clark has moved to change the structure of the next campaign by refusing to turn the party apparatus or campaign responsibility over to any group within the party. The party's first election campaign under his leadership will see a more decentralized approach utilizing the network of regional workers Clark has organized throughout the country.

"Joe is neither pro nor anti-Big Blue Machine," says Andre, "but we now know that there are people in the West and in the Atlantic region on hand to do a good job of managing a campaign on a regional basis." With Lowell Murray as the central coordinator, the party's campaign headquarters are expected to be in Ottawa and not Toronto as in the last two federal campaigns. Toronto and Ontario will be looked upon as a region as opposed to a headquarters. The reason for the shift in headquarters is largely symbolic. It should have the effect of playing down the impression that a handful of Toronto-based advertising wizards have the final say and at least give the appearance of the party having more control over its election machinery.

With plans well under way for the selling of Joe Clark, in the final analysis, he will simply be asking the voters to take him as he is. Before heading for Room 130-S on the night of 24 May 1977 to explain his party's poor showing in six federal by-elections, he remarked to the people around him, "It is better if I go down alone." Later he returned to his Centre Block office and asked Murray if he had seen any of his television appearance that night. Murray told him his hair looked ruffled on camera. That was truly a campaign chairman speaking, doubtless thinking of the impressionable voters. Yet even with a new hair style, a politician can be managed but he cannot be invented. In the end, Joe Clark is on his own.

Stornoway

Stornoway, the official residence of the Leader of Her Majesty's Loyal Opposition, was a lively place on the evening of 5 November 1976. Joe Clark and his wife Maureen had purchased a new stereo and were dancing with friends to some of Maureen's old numbers. The party ended at one o'clock the next morning when Maureen was rushed to Ottawa General Hospital, where she gave birth to a baby girl.

The arrival of Catherine Jane, now an active and inquisitive youngster, has added a dimension to life at Stornoway not usually associated with the austere household of the leader of the opposition. It has certainly changed the lifestyle of Maureen McTeer.

In many ways the wife of the leader of the opposition is a paradox. She is a feminist — witness her insistence on retaining her maiden name after her marriage to Clark — but more by example than by passionate speech-making. She can be an aggressive campaigner who on occasion does not hesitate to show her Irish temper. Yet she is no die-hard partisan, and in private is a woman of genuine warmth and humour. One thing is readily apparent: Maureen McTeer has a sense of showmanship and a personal flare that transcends her spirited exchanges with the media.

Maureen finally graduated from law school in June 1977, after failing her third-year law examination because she spent too much time on the campaign trail with her husband. She chose not to article right away and instead plans to devote her time to raising Catherine and assisting her husband with his career. Later on, however, she hopes to form an all-female law firm with three or four other women. "It's not just that we want to exclude males," she

The human side of political leadership. Joe Clark holds Catherine Jane at her christening on 24 December 1976.

says, "We were close all through law school and we know each other's interests, so it would be a fairly well-rounded law firm." But there is another reason for the move, somewhat more personal. "I don't want to work for someone else, because I need flexibility and you don't have flexibility unless you work for yourself."

Stornoway has not changed significantly since the Clarks arrived in 1976. Some of the decor is more modern but the Chinese silkcloth on the walls in the dining room, a carry-over from Mrs. Pearson's days, is still there. There's a 1902 globe of the world which the federal Department of Supply and Services dug out of storage. Only in the family room, as Maureen says, "it's all our furniture." Yet there is a distinctive western Canada flavour throughout the house. Typical is a painting in the hallway by O.N. Grandmaison, entitled "Moonlight Southern Alberta." At one end of the dining room is what Maureen describes as "the plant room" although, in her words, "I never really got into the plant thing because of a lack of time."

In the evenings, life at Stornoway is relaxed and informal. After dinner, Joe frequently goes to his study to catch up on correspondence he has brought home from the office. If it is a free evening, the couple may take in a movie. Maureen has seen the film "Rocky" three times and encouraged her husband to see it, because it is a lesson in how to overcome. Clark enjoyed "Rocky" but found "Network" too artificial. He watches John Denver's specials on television because "his programs are not slick" and he likes country music.

The deliberate avoidance of contrivance seems to permeate Clark's private life. He has two favourite clothing stores, Harry Pozy's Men's Wear in Ottawa and O'Connor's Men's Wear in Calgary. "He has a good idea of what he wants when he comes in," says Graham O'Connor. He is more conservative and formal in his clothes than his brother Peter whose law office is just a few doors down on Eighth Avenue in Calgary. Prior to the 1976 leadership convention Clark, characteristically, purchased a pin-striped navy blue suit and a double-breasted top coat.

However, in his eating habits, Joe Clark is venturesome. He can't be from Alberta and not like steak. But he experiments with new dishes. According to his wife, "If there is something interesting on the menu, he will usually try it." Among his favourites are lobster and fresh fish. He always declines potatoes, cold foods, sandwiches and hamburgers. "He never has a

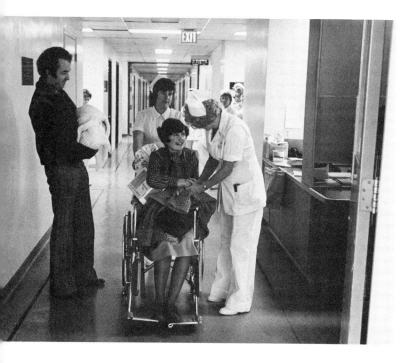

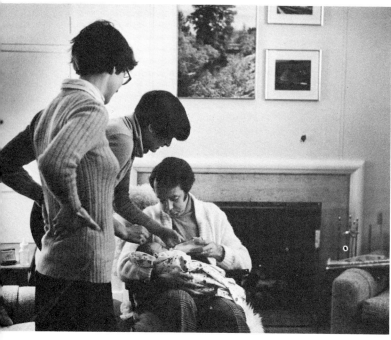

At home at Stornoway. Above: *Catherine plays in the dining room as her parents come in from the plant room to watch.* Top left: *Maureen leaves Ottawa Civic Hospital after the birth of her daughter.* Bottom left: *Organizing the leader of the opposition: Maureen helps Joe feed Catherine as former nanny, Hilary Davis, looks on.* Opposite: *A fast breakfast in the kitchen. Joe Clark snatches a few quiet minutes to read the paper every morning before he goes to the office;* Far right: *Maureen studying at home with Catherine on her knee. For now the days of studying law are over. Joe Clark shopping for his daughter. A tired Catherine Jane cuddles up to her mother before going up for her nap.*

Big Mac attack," say Maureen, "he likes green salads with his mother's dressing which I have never been able to do and one of these days I will get the exact recipe." The reason for Clark's egg nog breakfasts in the morning is to line his stomach for the heavy coffee-drinking day ahead of him. He drinks coffee almost incessantly, leaving him with stomach pains at the end of the day. "I think it's because that is all they have there," says Maureen, "so he'll say bring me a cup of coffee. And when you run on a tight schedule you are often very tired, so coffee recharges you."

Joe and Maureen differ in their reading habits and Clark is more escapist than his wife, preferring murder mysteries and auto magazines although, perhaps inevitably for a politician, the book shelves in his study at Stornoway are filled with works such as George Grant's *Lament for a Nation.* His wife is fond of biographies in general and was particularly impressed with Golda Meir's autobiography. Among other forms of relaxation for them are cross-country skiing, cycling and walking.

The casual atmosphere at Stornoway is reflected in their relaxed style of dress. When he arrives home, Clark generally changes into his favourite pale yellow cardigan, slacks and slippers. "I never change," laughs Maureen. For her, it is generally sweaters and slacks or, in the warm weather, light dresses and ensembles. For travelling and campaigning, winter and summer, she prefers suits.

The leader's wife is introducing a new style of entertaining to the nation's capital. Western barbecues, costume parties, fancy-dress balls, skating and skiing parties are to her liking. She finds the cocktail circuit tedious and dreary and wants to break away from that traditional mode of entertaining. This new scheme is actually an extension of her feeling that Canadians should focus more on the various regions of the country and less on the Toronto-Ottawa-Montreal nexus. The theme is a familiar one to anyone who listened to Joe Clark's speeches during his rise to the top of the Conservative party. Maureen's plan is to entertain artists, writers and other Canadians from varying backgrounds across Canada at Stornoway. "They have a view of Canada and a feeling for the country which is different from us, because ours is often very political."

Considering the size of the two-story mansion and its attractive grounds, Stornoway's staff is small. While she finished law school Maureen relied on nanny Hilary Davis, a pleasant, reserved young woman who left Stornoway in May 1977. The responsibilities of the nanny, who saw her role

Joe Clark tries to spend as much time as he can with his young daughter, and whenever possible he will be home to see her at bedtime.

The habitual coffee drinker.

as the traditional British one of caring for children, were a source of mild tension in the household. Maureen explained that she would look to the nanny to perform housekeeping duties while she spent time with Catherine, but somehow the arrangement did not prove satisfactory. Now the Clarks have a full-time housekeeper, Pauline Cook, a native of Newfoundland, who lives in a self-contained apartment above the garage at Stornoway. There is also a gardener who visits regularly to tend the flowers and thick hedges at Stornoway.

In his book *Recollections of People, Press and Politics,* Grattan O'Leary recounts how Stornoway was purchased in the early 1950s from a daughter of Sir George Perley for $40,000. It was felt that the leader of the opposition should have a more prestigious home than the apartment in the Roxborough where George Drew had lived. So O'Leary and a group of his business friends bought Stornoway and, over the years, spent $175,000 to maintain it. In 1970 the federal government assumed the upkeep of the historic house, which had been built in 1914 and named by one of its early owners for her ancestral home in the Hebrides. The federal Department of Public Works picked up the tab for the $20,000 spent on renovations and furnishings when the Clarks moved into the official residence.

Since 1948, Stornoway has been occupied by George Drew, Lester Pearson, John Diefenbaker, Robert Stanfield and now Joe Clark. If you go by Stornoway's track record as a staging area for preparing its residents for higher things, then Joe Clark has an even chance of making it down the road to the prime minister's residence. Two of the four previous occupants of Stornoway, Lester Pearson and John Diefenbaker, eventually ended up at 24 Sussex Drive. If Clark does become prime minister, swimming lessons could be in store for him or the most celebrated pool since Babylon could go to waste. As Clark explained during an interview on national television in April 1976, "We're going to try to take some lessons that will make sure that I can swim in the pool." As a youngster, Clark nearly drowned while fishing with his father in High River. Apparently, the water still scares him. When asked if he swims these days, he replies, "I sink." At 24 Sussex Drive, that would never do.

L'Avenir

The time is 8:05 p.m. on the night of 24 May 1977. The place is the Centre Block office of the leader of the opposition. Results from six federal by-elections, five in Quebec and one in Prince Edward Island, are starting to come in. A television set has been installed in the office so that Clark can watch the returns. With him are his wife, who has campaigned strenuously in the by-elections, Bill Neville, John Laschinger and Lowell Murray. Suspense grips the room. A lot is at stake on this one night. Clark is looking for a breakthrough in Quebec and has devoted much of his time as leader to campaigning in the province. Moreover, the party wants to show Ontario that it has a foothold there. Because Ontario views itself as the centre of the nation, the Conservatives feel that, in the current concern for the country's unity, the province will only support a political party that has demonstrable strength in French Canada. So this night also is an opportunity for the Conservative leader to show Ontario, the linchpin of Confederation, that his party cannot be counted out in Quebec and that the Liberals no longer own the national unity issue.

The returns from the riding of Malpeque in Prince Edward Island set a sombre tone for the evening. For twenty-five years the Tories had held the seat, but Conservative Ian MacQuarrie narrowly lost to the Liberal Donald Wood. While he tried to take it in his stride, Clark was noticeably distressed at the PEI results. He knew the Quebec seats were long shots, but Malpeque had been a party stronghold. Beside campaigning in the riding himself, Clark had persuaded John Diefenbaker to visit the province hoping to hold the riding. Now Clark was on the phone trying to console the defeated

The evening of 24 May 1977 was a long, dispiriting vigil. Watching the federal by-election results with Clark in his office are, from left to right: John Laschinger, Lowell Murray, Bill Neville, Ian Green and Donald Doyle.

candidate. "Keep your running shoes on," he said on the phone to Ian MacQuarrie, indicating the party plans to run the candidate in the next election.

After the Malpeque results are in, Clark turns to the three party organizers in the room and quips: "What a life, I remember Calgary South." (In the 1967 Alberta provincial election, Clark had contested that seat against Socred candidate Art Dixon and had come within 461 votes of winning. One political pollster at the time, when asked by Clark what he thought his chances of winning were, is said to have replied: "Well, there was, after all, a virgin birth." Clark had hoped to send the pessimistic pollster a telegram saying, "Come to Bethlehem and see" but never got the chance.)

As the by-election returns are announced, CBC television commentators are extrapolating the implications of the results for Clark's future as leader of the Conservative party. The Horner defection, Claude Wagner's disaffection and the loss of Malpeque, in the eyes of the commentators, are certain to cause spasms within Tory ranks and Clark's leadership could be on the line. There is silence in the office as everyone listens.

Don McNeil, former Ottawa and Washington correspondent, is doing most of the speculating on the future of Clark's leadership. What irks Clark most are the commentators' suggestions that the Conservatives had forged an alliance with the Parti Québecois hoping to capitalize on separatist sentiment. That night McNeil was, in Clark's eyes, a commentator "with authority but without facts."

As the long evening wore on, it soon became apparent that the party was to be shut out in all six ridings. The Liberals took five of the six. Gilles Caouette, son of former Creditiste leader Réal Caouette, held Témiscamingue for his party.

The agony is almost over except for the leader. He has yet to face the television cameras and explain what happened to the organization he is building in Quebec. There was hardly a ray of sunshine. Yet Clark knew he had to make an appearance in Room 130-S. What was there to salvage from the by-election returns? The answer was not much.

Laschinger, Murray and Neville huddled in front of the fireplace in the office reviewing the figures and pooling their wisdom, hoping to find a silver lining. Watching them with a slight smile on his face, Clark sat for a moment on the large desk in the office, while his fingers fiddled with a paper clip. Laschinger tells Clark to "take the high road," adding "It's time for a little humour." Neville wants a straightforward approach. "I'd play it straight," he says, "We know we have an uphill fight in Quebec." Then Lowell Murray's sense of humour begins to show as he and Clark train their sights on the CBC commentators suggesting that the Conservatives and Parti Québecois were in bed with each other. "What we should say," Murray says, "was that if the PQ had been working for us we would have won. Obviously by the vote, they were all working for Trudeau." Clark responds: "I think that might have possibilities." Shortly afterward, Clark leaves the office to face the reporters.

The night of 24 May 1977 had been disappointing. The only glimmer of hope for the Tories was that their share of the popular vote in the five

Top: *Clark and his wife watch the disappointing results coming in from Quebec. Smiles were hard to come by on the evening of 24 May 1977.*

Bottom: *Clark and Maureen stare at the TV screen as the results come in. In the foreground Laschinger prepares to analyse the returns.*

Quebec ridings had increased to 26 per cent from 15 per cent in 1974. But that was not substantial enough. As Clark told newsmen, "Quebec is tough ground for us." After the by-elections, the party still had only three members of Parliament from Quebec. Because the Conservative caucus remained predominantly from English Canada, Clark, as party leader, would have to continue to serve as a counterweight to ensure that policy positions and debate in caucus considered those interests in the country which are not directly represented.

The choice of Quebec City for the party's biennial policy convention no doubt was an attempt to dispel the views of those skeptical of the party's future in Quebec and to show Clark's determination to establish a federal alternative in the province. The theme of the conference in early November 1977 was "Canada at the Crossroads"; in the leader's view, it was to be the kick-off to the Tories' next election campaign. Certainly how Clark emerged from the convention would go a long way in determining the party's chances in the next election. The convention was deliberately orchestrated to avoid open policy conflicts such as the disputes which arose in the late 1960s over the party's approach to French-English relations. No votes were held on policy resolutions and the workshop sessions dealt only with broad policy

On the phone to defeated candidates.

questions. Duncan Edmonds, Clark's chief policy adviser, put it in a nutshell when he observed that "the objective was not to make mistakes, and to get the party to ratify its choice of leader." The outcome could hardly have been more favourable for Clark.

The conference dealt early with the most important item on the agenda, namely, the vote on a leadership review. Under the party's constitution, the some 1,500 delegates had a right, by a simple majority, to call a leadership convention if they desired. There were 1,031 votes cast in the leadership review vote and an overwhelming 959 were against holding a leadership convention. In effect, more than 93 per cent of the voting delegates expressed their approval of Clark's leadership. The melancholy days of spring were now passed.

What to tell the media? Laschinger, Murray, Neville and Doyle try to salvage something politically from the dismal evening.

As he stood before his party on the opening night of the conference, the delegates saw a mature politician rather than the untried young man of two years ago. With poise and ease, almost nonchalantly, Clark dealt with the questions put to him at a delegate bearpit session — questions ranging from nuclear fusion to multiculturism. Gone was the awkwardness of his early public appearances as leader: the anxious manner, the stilted gestures, the obvious and intense partisanship. Now, in Quebec City, Clark radiated self-possession. To the assembled faithful he obviously had stature.

Clark himself is aware of this transition. "I've become more assertive of my own preferences. There was a time when I was being a balancer and try-ing to bring people together, but now I am more inclined to say this is the way it should be done." The candidate who had gone into the 1976 leadership convention with the fewest enemies and emerged with the most friends had consolidated his position in the caucus and the party, and could now prepare for a federal election campaign.

Clark's success at Quebec City would give the Conservative leader leverage in his dealings with the business-industrial community. The realization that the party was solidly behind him should help him also in the recruitment of Conservative candidates for the election campaign. Financial leaders, for the most part, had been reluctant to accept Clark as the credible leader of an alternative government. They were concerned when they saw the disruptions in the Conservative caucus; all too obvious was Clark's difficulty in his own constituency, and Jack Horner's noisy departure. And then, as Duncan Edmonds explained, "the polls went through the floor" following the PQ victory. Clark has had little experience of the corporate world. Edmonds has urged Clark to be less dogmatic in his dealings with the business community but to try to show a general awareness of the difficulties facing them. In any event, Clark could now meet members of the business world on terms more favourable to him. With his party seemingly united and his hold on the leadership consolidated, he would have to be perceived as the logical alternative by those disenchanted with the economic policies of the Liberal government. "Real progress had been made with the business community," says Edmonds, "but it is still an upward battle. We have to get across Clark's management skills and his good sense of Canada."

Clark's "good sense of Canada" and his concept of her past borders on romanticism. Any conversation about the history of the country soon drifts around to Wallace Stegner, an American, but, in Clark's words, "a perceptive spokesman of the Western idea." Stegner's likening history to "a pontoon bridge" with every man walking and working "at its building end" appeals to Clark, because he feels the words help to explain the settlement of Canada. "It's the idea," he says, "of going out into something not quite sure, building out into space and you're adding on to something, doing something new and yet doing it in a way connected with the past." This sense of building, according to Clark, is one of the differences between Canada and the United States. Whereas the United States tried to develop new values on a new continent, Canada sought to remodel old ones on a new continent. Wars might have defined other countries but Clark is quick to point out that "our major events have been building events such as the railway and the seaway, or the 1956 pipeline debate, a major debate in Canadian history, in

Maureen tastes the sourness of political defeat. Joe studies the election returns on television.

134

Over: *A leader triumphant. Clark receiving his party's endorsation of his leadership in Quebec City in November 1977. The theme of the policy convention was "Canada at the Crossroads."*

part, because it was related to building." Clark saw the most recent pipeline debate in that tradition and concludes that the concept of building is natural for "a continental country, a big country."

As 1977 came to a close, opinion polls showed the Liberals dropping in popularity with 42 per cent of the decided voters and the Tories with 34 per cent — almost identical to the positions held by the two parties on election day in 1974. The Liberal decline was blamed on rising unemployment and increased living costs, two economic factors which, along with national unity, would be central to the next federal election campaign. As the country looked to 1978, some confusion still rested in the voters' minds about Clark. With the Liberal government staggering from one ineptitude to another, was Clark the strong leader needed to get the country on its feet again? What did he *really* stand for?

"Perhaps the best thing Joe Clark had going for him," wrote Geoffrey Stevens, "when he was elected leader of the Conservative party in February, 1976 was that he was not Pierre Trudeau. Who Mr. Clark was, where he had come from, what he had done in the past, and what he promised to stand for in the future, were less important than the fact that the country was disenchanted with the Government and the Prime Minister." Whether Clark's strength as a political leader in 1976 — his sharp distinctiveness from Pierre Trudeau — would serve him well in 1978 remained to be seen.

Certainly, in the Conservative party under Clark the electorate have a clear alternative to the Liberal administration. The belief in Trudeau as the only man who could negotiate with Quebec and hold the country together — a view espoused by many political commentators across the country following Lévesque's victory — has begun to falter. Since the end of 1977 the media have treated Clark more kindly and given his speeches and his performance in the House more attention.

Throughout it all Clark, seemingly undaunted, has plodded ahead, meeting the electorate and methodically building up the voters' perceptions of his abilities. His past experience tells him that the key to winning lies in a strong party organization. He knows all too well the Conservatives' propensity for snatching defeat from the jaws of victory. He also knows he may never get another chance to move into 24 Sussex Drive. The election campaign will be the greatest challenge of Joe Clark's career.